HE WAS

*Alzheimer's was his battle.
It was not who he was.*

Denise C. LeBlanc

He Was
Copyright © 2019 Denise C. LeBlanc
All rights reserved

Book cover design by Olivia Sanders,
Grandpa Ronnie Carlin's "Livvy"
Editing by Tom Bird Retreats, Inc.

No part of this book may be reproduced in any form or by any electronic or mechanical means, including information storage and retrieval systems, without prior permission in writing from the author. The only exception is by a reviewer, who may quote short excerpts in a review.

Some names and identifying details have been changed to protect the privacy of the individuals.

Denise LeBlanc books are available for order through Amazon.com
Visit my website: www.HeWasthebook.com
Twitter: @HeWasTheBook
Facebook: www.facebook.com/hewasthebook

Printed in the United States of America
First Printing: February 2019
Published by Tom Bird Retreats, Inc.

Paperback ISBN: 978-1-62747-398-9
Ebook ISBN: 978-1-62747-336-1

This book is dedicated to my mother, Donna Carlin.

*She was his childhood sweetheart,
his faithful and loving wife of 54 years,
and his caregiver throughout this long, painful battle.
She is a perky little ray of sunshine, who is always on the go,
who is loved by many, and who loves the Lord.
She had incredible strength to take care of my Dad
and to watch him disappear before her eyes.
He loved her so much. She was his heart.
She Was and Is my beautiful Mother.
I Love You,
Mom.*

*To Doug –
Thank you for always supporting me and for being my
biggest fan. You encourage me to follow my heart and
you always see potential in me when I do not see it
myself. Thank you for always being proud of me.
I love you and I am proud to be your wife.*

Acknowledgments

I have the most amazing family. I watched as we banded together to make the best of the time we had left with my dad. I then watched as they supported me through the process of documenting his battle.

Thank you to my sister Julie for your gentle kindness in caring for Daddy. You were the best at bringing him back to a place of peace. Thank you for helping me remember details and for editing the early drafts. Thank you for being the best sister on the planet.

Thank you to my daughter Lauren for being my heart. Thank you for reading and editing and sharing your emotions throughout this process. I am so blessed to have you as my smart and beautiful daughter. Grandpa was so proud of you and your choice to be an accountant like him.

Thank you to my niece Olivia for creating the beautiful cover of this book. Grandpa sure loved his Livvy. He would have loved to watch you grow as you start your amazing career.

Thank you to my in-laws, John and Fronnie LeBlanc. You have loved me like your own and I can't begin to thank you enough for raising such an amazing son. Thank you for reading and editing the early draft. Also, thank you for loving my dad with kindness and respect.

Thank you to my sista-cuz, Cristi Carlin Tidwell. Our journey to Sedona to write our books was nothing short of magical. The same can be said for our journey through life. I'm so proud of you and I thank you for always being there for me.

Thank you to my precious friend, Annella Metoyer. You were my mentor first and then became my dearest friend. Your encouragement was so important to me, but your bravery to step out on this author journey first was inspiring. You gave me the confidence I needed to do something I never thought was possible.

Thank you to Tom Bird. You have equipped thousands of people to achieve their dreams of being an author. I am honored to be one of your many.

Table of Contents

Foreword................................... ix
Introduction xi
Chapter 1 – An Elephant Never Forgets 1
Chapter 2 – Who Is Alzheimer's? 8
Chapter 3 – Who Was He? 15
Chapter 4 – The Stages Of Grief................. 19
Chapter 5 – Why Did I Write This Book?......... 23
Chapter 6 – Did We Miss Something?............. 26
Chapter 7 – Paradise In Sour Lake 30
Chapter 8 – And On Stage #3, We Have Reality 37
Chapter 9 – No More Denying 43
Chapter 10 – I've Seen This Before 46
Chapter 11 – The Talk......................... 49
Chapter 12 – The Truth........................ 52
Chapter 13 – The Battle Begins.................. 61
Chapter 14 – Obsessions And Fixations 69
Chapter 15 – Speaking With No Filter............ 79
Chapter 16 – His Fears And Mine 85

Chapter 17 – Next To The Last Trip To Heaven 93

Chapter 18 – A Glimmer Of Hope Tarnished. 100

Chapter 19 – New People In The House 107

Chapter 20 – All The Daddies I Loved 110

Chapter 21 – Moving To Rose Street. 114

Chapter 22 – He's Gone 122

Chapter 23 – Saying Goodbye. 127

Chapter 24 – He Was. 131

Chapter 25 – What A Beautiful Day For A Funeral . . .137

Chapter 26 – I Am. 139

Epilogue – Things I've Learned 141

About The Author. 145

Endnotes. 147

Foreword

Getting spanked by mistake has been a source of laughter for us the past few years. Of course, at the time, Dad was attempting to establish punishment on the sister who didn't drink the unclaimed chocolate milk. One of us lied. One of us told the truth. We both got a spanking. As an adult, Dad was still apologizing for me being the victim of my milk-hating sister, but it resulted in laughing and forgiveness way long past. He was big-hearted.

It's a privilege to be writing the foreword to Denise's memoir. She opens her heart with those who either already know or soon will learn the pain of Alzheimer's. Denise is my sister, best friend, ear to share my ideas, and fellow dreamer. She was also my momma-bear partner as we fiercely protected our father's well-being.

She knows first-hand the good, bad, and super ugliness of a journey through Alzheimer's. She points out how medical information is necessary. But the club you've never intended to join is so important as you become dependent upon the other members' advice. She regularly meets countless souls walking this journey with their parents and expresses just the right words they need to hear.

He Was will be that friend who says they understand and is longed for during times when you don't know what to do. Just even knowing how to respond to mixed-up conversations helped reduce stress with both us and Dad. You'll be glad to know you're not alone. Meet Ronnie, who loved telling stores, and see the gift he passed down to his daughter. Get your tissues, coffee, and take a breath. The words will be like sunshine as they warm your bones and lighten your path.

– Julie Carlin Sanders,
Ronnie Carlin's Youngest Daughter

Introduction

He Was Ronald Mason Carlin
He Was a grandson
He Was a son
He Was a brother
He Was a cousin
He Was a friend
He Was a Christian
He Was a Golden Gloves boxer
He Was a drummer
He Was a class president
He Was a husband
He Was a hunter
He Was a golfer
He Was a fisherman
He Was a jitterbug dancer
He Was a rose gardener
He Was a Certified Public Accountant
He Was a teacher
He Was smart
He Was funny
He Was honest
He Was faithful
He Was Godly
He Was kind
He Was loved
He Was My Daddy

Chapter One

An Elephant Never Forgets

"**H**ey, Shug! This is your Pop. My computer is fouled up again."

This daily call from my dad started as they all did. "*Hey, Shug. This is your Pop.*" He called me, my mom, and my sister, "Shug" which was short for "Sugar." He would explain what he couldn't do on his computer, and I would try to help him over the phone. But today I couldn't understand what he was trying to explain.

He told me, "The lady that works for Harold is here. I'm trying to print his tax return, but it's all fouled up."

I asked him, "Is Connie over there?"

"No. It's the lady that works for Harold."

Connie had been Harold's secretary for many, many years. Why wasn't he saying her name?

Since I lived a few blocks away and I was home early that day, I told him I'd come over and fix the problem. I had no idea this would be the day my life changed forever.

I walked in the unlocked, back door of my parent's house and went straight to the office.

There it was.

The big elephant we had been avoiding and walking around for months.

This time it had shown up in front of someone outside the family. As I write that sentence, I realize it had been obvious to many outside the family. This was the first time the outside and inside stared the elephant in the face at the same time.

Today the elephant was a desk covered in about four reams of paper, thousands of pages of various tax forms and information, strung all over his desk and floor. He was calmer than I expected. As if the mess were no big deal. However, I knew it was a big deal by the look on Connie's face as she peered at me over the mounds of paper.

The problem was that the printer wouldn't print. I fixed it by closing the paper tray.

Dad said, "I finished Harold's tax return. The tax program was messing up and doubling numbers, so I plugged the right numbers and wrote a note to the IRS on the return."

Connie's wide-eyed, nervous smile let me know that she understood, as did I, that it was not okay, and he was not okay.

I asked him to let me sit down in his chair to see if I could find what was causing the problem. He said, "Sure." I found the problem immediately. He was typing information in two different places when it should have been entered in one. After more than 40 years of preparing taxes, his making this novice mistake was out of place.

Since this was something he should have known and because Connie was so uncomfortably smiling, sadly trying to communicate to me with her eyes without saying anything, I asked if I could review the tax return, to "*brush up on my tax prep skills.*" Uncharacteristically, he said "Okay." He said he needed to go to the little boy's room and walked out of the office.

I couldn't make eye contact with Connie because the elephant was blocking my view. I was afraid to speak because I was worried she had seen it, also. I was afraid because I knew she had seen it and I didn't know what to do next.

Sweet Connie got up from her chair in front of the desk and carefully made her way past all the discarded papers on the floor.

I froze.

I couldn't breathe.

I wouldn't have this conversation.

I stared at the screen as if I couldn't see her, pretending to read the return. She put her hand on my shoulder and asked, "Is your Daddy okay?" I never looked up or spoke. I just shook my head "No," as tears filled my eyes. There were no words.

The elephant was sitting on my chest.

It was sitting on my heart.

I had to acknowledge its existence.

Daddy came back in the room and started digging through his desk drawers, pulling out old pictures of deer from his property, and laughing as he showed them to us. He was oblivious to the situation.

I reworked the tax return, printed it and gave it to Connie. As I walked her out to the front porch, she hugged me. Her sweet words and hug should have comforted me, but instead, they crushed my whole being.

My mind was screaming.

All I could think was, *"He's going to die."*

Reality hit hard.

"My dad is gone."

"Who is this precious man next to me and how will we move forward?

Does he know there is something wrong?

Is he scared?

After always being my strength and protector, am I now going to become his?"

"God, Please Stop This! Please don't make him live... and die like this!"

As I tried to clean up his office a little bit, I made small talk with him about tax returns and his plans for the rest of his clients. The words were hard to form and seemed to be stuck in my throat, requiring me to choke and force them out. My eyes stung, yet I refused to cry. There was no way I would do that to him. My mind was like an exploding planet.

He showed me pictures, laughed, and told me stories about things stacked on his desk. He was enjoying my company, but I can't say I was enjoying his. It was so much more than that. It was an acute awareness that I needed to remember every second of every minute of our time together from now on because it would end one day.

At that moment, he and I were in two different worlds. However, the unseen, beautiful bond of a Daddy and a Daughter was stronger than ever. It was the strongest feeling swirling around in my broken heart.

"Not HIM!"

"Please Lord, let this be something minor and fixable, that we can laugh about later."

I knew it wasn't.

I went home that day to my husband and collapsed. I was crushed and defeated by the elephant. It had mauled me and stomped me into the ground. I grieved as if my Dad had died. As a matter of fact, the Daddy I had always known was already gone. It wasn't the first time I had seen a glimpse of what was happening to him, but it was the first time I allowed myself to acknowledge the horrible truth.

He was gone... But not.

*"What will happen next?
What do we do? Do we tell him?
Does Mom know?"*

Again, I couldn't breathe. I hate the elephant. I hate it with all that is within me. Why did it have to show up at our family's front door? And, how does our family survive this next chapter in our lives knowing that one of us will not survive?

Every cell in my body is sad. I vow to tell him I love him, every single day. Every single day for the rest of his life. He may eventually forget everything he knew, but my Dad will never forget how much he is loved.

Daddy had done tax returns for people since he was in college and had lots of clients that he worked with for most of his life. When I was a kid, I liked tax season because my sister, Julie, and I got presents. He didn't always charge everyone for his services, so he would barter or do some pro bono. Some clients would give him a meal for our family at their restaurant, or they would send home something for Julie and me. One year my sister and I got ceramic, 12-inch tall, E.T. banks made by one of his clients. They had our names on them. They were a little strange, but I still have mine. One client sent him a Hickory Farms meat and cheese gift box every year. I would sit on the back porch and share the meat sticks and cheese spreads with our dog, Patches.

The other thing I liked about tax season was watching him work. His office was his domain. My sister and I would invade his space and watch him do his thing. His fingers flew on the 10-key adding machine, and the sound it made was staccato and in perfect rhythm. He would let the tape run the full length of the roll, then he'd rewind it backward and run new calculations on the back. Such an accountant. He was always frugal.

His office smelled like pencil lead and eraser, mixed with pipe tobacco. When we were kids, the office was in a musty back add-on to the garage, so it smelled a little earthy.

He liked to listen to music when he worked. He played it loud. He would pull his drumsticks out of the desk and play along with one of his favorites, using his pencil sharpener as a cymbal. He played well and would laugh the whole time he performed. He tried to teach us how to hold the sticks and play, but neither my sister nor I had the talent. He kept two sets of sticks in the bottom drawer. One that he played with and one from his friend that committed suicide in junior high *"over a girl."* He would tell us the story about the sticks sometimes. He would be sad as he reminisced. Then, he would go back to playing with the music.

I always loved watching him work. He was smart. When I grew up, I wanted to have a desk and clients and an adding machine and enjoy what I did as much as he enjoyed what he did. Eventually, I got my wish.

The rest of that tax season was brutal. Daddy had lost a few clients over the past few years because they had lost confidence in his ability. He was making mistakes. It really hurt his feelings when people would take their returns to someone else. He didn't see any of the issues we were all starting to notice. He felt bewildered and betrayed.

I worked for a CPA during tax season the previous year. I wasn't sure why the CPA asked me to come to work, but I now know why. God knew Daddy would need my help. For the remainder of the season, I did the returns for his clients. He didn't want them to know I was doing the work and he would check the forms and sign-off on them. My heart was heavy, and my mind was focused. I had to do a good job and ask him questions because I knew soon he would not know the answers.

He sat in the den, eating dinner and watching TV, while I did the personal returns for him and Mom. I knew things would never be the same and I wanted to cry the entire time. Just last year he would never have gotten up from his desk to let me take over his work or to find his mistake. It was so out of character. So not him. He knew what he was doing and would take care of his business. He didn't need my help.

But, things had now changed. And, he did need my help.

I screamed in my head, *"Get in here and do this return! This is all a bad dream!"*

Then I'd hear him laugh at something he was watching, and I'd think to myself, *"This is not a dream. Dear God, what am I going to do?"*

Tears sat in my eyelids during these internal conversations. Thankfully they stayed there until I got in the car.

My family now lived in a new and rapidly changing world.

Stupid elephant.

Chapter Two

Who Is Alzheimer's?

You know the scene in *Back to the Future* where Marty is failing at his attempt to unite his parents at the "Under the Sea" dance? When he realized things weren't working out as planned, he looked at the picture of his family that he was holding and saw the images of him, his brother, and his sister begin to fade away, as if they never existed.

This is what Alzheimer's disease does to its victims. It slowly erases their memories and moves them backward in time. They forget who they were and forget who they loved.

I wrote this book backward. I started near the middle of my Dad's journey where the acknowledgment of his condition occurred. Then I wrote the day he died and the funeral. Next, I wrote the weeks leading up to his death. This wasn't on purpose. It was the way the story was telling itself as I put it on paper. Backward in time. Just like Alzheimer's carries our loved ones. They come to a specific moment in their life and then start slowly regressing backward rather than progressing forward.

My daddy was forgetting who he was. He didn't remember that he loved Dairy Queen Blizzards even though he had one every day for more than a decade. He stopped liking the chicken soup at a local restaurant that was always his favorite. He also had a hard time remembering all the people at the Christmas dinner table and their names. He knew they were family and that he loved them. He just couldn't place their names or their relationships to the others. He started asking what to order at restaurants.

He would ask, "What do I get here?"
Mom would tell him.
"Do I like it?"
"Oh yes! It's one of your favorites."
"I do? Hmmm," in an "O*k, I guess I believe you*" huff.

A person with Alzheimer's loses his or her freedom long before they lose their life.

Want to drive? Denied!
Want to have a meaningful conversation? Denied!
Want to be independent and go and do what you want to do? Denied!
Want to enjoy the hobbies you developed for years and years? Denied!
Want to remember your grandkids? Denied!

There are three significant scales describing the progression of Alzheimer's disease. One is the Global Deterioration Scale (GDS)[1], developed by Dr. Barry Reisberg. Another is used by the Alzheimer's Association and is defined in three general stages – Mild, Moderate, and Severe[2]. When you put the two forms of measurement together, stages one, two, and three are considered "Mild." Stages four and five are labeled as "Moderate." And, stages six and seven are "Severe."

In addition to the scales mentioned above, the Mayo Clinic has a five-stage description of how the disease progresses. The five stages are pre-clinical Alzheimer's disease, mild cognitive impairment due to Alzheimer's disease, mild dementia due to Alzheimer's, moderate dementia due to Alzheimer's and severe dementia due to Alzheimer's.[3]

My View of Stages Combined

Global Deterioration Scale	Alzheimer's Association	Mayo Clinic
Stage One	Mild	Pre-clinical Alzheimer's
Stage Two	Mild	
Stage Three	Mild	Mild cognitive impairment due to Alzheimer's
Stage Four	Moderate	Mild dementia due to Alzheimer's
Stage Five	Moderate	Moderate dementia due to Alzheimer's
Stage Six	Severe	Severe dementia due to Alzheimer's
Stage Seven	Severe	

In hindsight, we saw such a distinction between each stage of the disease that I will be using the GDS, seven-stage measurement as my frame of reference.

But, please remember I am not a doctor. I'm relating our personal experiences, the way we viewed the progression of this disease and our interpretation of the three scales.

Stage One of Alzheimer's disease is undetectable by the victim and by those around them. It is referred to as pre-clinical Alzheimer's disease. There are no outward indications of the disease's progression. However, deposits of beta-amyloid proteins are starting to form within the brain. This stage can last for several years. It's not until enough of these deposits are present, causing disruption to the brain's ability to function correctly, that Alzheimer's disease is detectable outside of a few medical tests. Even then, the tests are indicators of risks and not a diagnosis of the disease.

Stage Two is difficult to detect due to a very mild decline of the victim. Memory lapses are generally seen as "old age" and not attributed to any other underlying issue. However, the individual may be experiencing problems with remembering names and words more frequently than someone else in their same age group. Most people will not notice anything unusual, either in themselves or in their loved one. The person is continuing to live a normal life, both socially and professionally.

Stage Three is where the disease rears its ugly head to be seen by the outside world. Personally, I see this as the *"elephant in the room"* stage. Cognitive impairments, although slight, become noticeable to loved ones and can be detected by physicians utilizing memory tests. Individuals may have a difficult time remembering names, finding the right words in conversations, and recalling where they have left personal possessions; such as their wallet and keys. Also, they may have difficulty organizing and planning tasks. Anxiety may begin to appear as the person struggles to overcome lapses in memory and cognitive issues. It is a difficult time for the individual, as they may be having problems performing work tasks that were previously routine. They may be feeling embarrassment when they fail to recall the name of someone they know.

Stage Four is marked by a moderate decline in the individual's abilities, and symptoms of the disease are now evident. Complexity in daily routine becomes challenging for the person to navigate. Paying bills and multi-step tasks require assistance, and they have difficulty in making sound judgments. All this confusion can cause a person to become withdrawn or irritable. And, understandably so. Finding the correct words to express themselves can be painfully difficult and sometimes impossible. This is where the term "*dementia*" enters. According to the book Mayo Clinic on Alzheimer's Disease, "*... severe memory loss, confusion, personality changes and the inability to perform routine tasks are known collectively as dementia and result from abnormal brain processes, not age.*"[4]

Stage Five is still considered moderate decline, but now the individual requires more help with daily activities. They are more confused as their brains are succumbing to the atrophy caused by the overabundance of beta-amyloid proteins. They find it difficult to dress appropriately for the day, although some people can still bathe and perform self-care for themselves. Incontinence in bladder and bowel functions require the use of adult diapers and present the need for assistance with personal hygiene. The individual is now becoming significantly confused. They usually remember family members' faces but may have difficulty recalling their names. The individual can usually recall stories about events in their past, but not be able to tell you the day of the week or what they did yesterday. Due to the decline in their cognitive reasoning, they are increasingly confused and are unable to make sound judgments. They may begin to wander because of restlessness or confusion. They may begin to be suspicious of caregivers and loved ones. Suspicion and confusion can lead to aggression. The individual's personality may be much different than it was before Alzheimer's disease took over.

Stage Six is the beginning of a severe decline and is like Stage Five except that the symptoms are now much more pronounced. The individual may no longer recognize friends and family, except those who are the closest and most frequently seen. They lose the details of their pasts. If they weren't already incontinent, they would lose bladder and bowel control during this stage. They require assistance with some functions of daily living, such as bathing and dressing. Their personality continues to change, as does their behavior and reactions to situations. Professional help may be required due to the physical and mental strain being experienced by the caregiver.

Stage Seven is the final stage of this cruel disease. The individual can no longer communicate in a meaningful manner or respond to their environment. They may become unable to walk or sit up without support. Muscles no longer reflex normally and may become rigid. As they near death, they depend on a caregiver for all daily activities.

Alzheimer's is no respecter of persons. It is indiscriminate as to who will be its next victim. It affects male and female, rich and poor, elite and ordinary, educated and self-made. It steals the essence of the person it attacks, and it is brutal and unyielding in its assault. It has taken down presidents and prime ministers. It has triumphed over generals and housewives. And the saddest part of all ... it always wins.

The statistics found on the Alzheimer's Association website are staggering.[5]

- Alzheimer's disease is the 6th leading cause of death in the United States.
- The number of Americans living with Alzheimer's is approximately 5.7 million.

  - 5.5 million of these people are age 65 and older.
  - This means 1 in 10 people over the age of 65 has Alzheimer's dementia.

- Every 65 seconds, someone in the United States develops Alzheimer's. This is expected to increase to every 33 seconds by 2050.

- Almost two-thirds of Americans with Alzheimer's are women.
- Older African-Americans are about twice as likely to have Alzheimer's or other dementias as older Caucasians.
- Hispanics are about one and a half times as likely to have Alzheimer's or other dementias as older Caucasians.

And remember: with 5.7 million people suffering from Alzheimer's disease, there must be at least twice that many people loving them and seeing them suffer. Victims are our grandparents, our parents, our siblings, and our friends. We love them and want to understand what is happening to them, although we truly can't. All we can do is be there to help them navigate this scary and treacherous road.

Chapter Three

Who Was He?

My dad, Ronald M. Carlin, or "Ronnie," as he was called, was born September 18, 1943. He was the blond haired, blue-eyed middle son of five boys. His wife, Donna, caught his eye when he was six years old, and she was five. She was wearing a blue and white polka-dot dress, at the First Baptist Church of Groves, Texas. They were in junior high band together when my mom wrote in her diary, *"Today I met a cute boy named Ronnie Carlin."* After dating through junior high and high school, they married on November 29, 1963. In August 1966, they had their first daughter. This is where I join the story. My sister came along in May 1969.

Ours was a typical, everyday kind of family. Nothing special, but average in every sense of the word. Our mom and dad were stable parents. Our dad went to work every day during the week, mowed the grass, and went fishing or hunting on the weekends. Our mom was a stay-at-home mom who made cookies when it rained and taught Vacation Bible School. Her favorite pastime was, and still is, shopping. They each had their hobbies and did their own thing, but at night, we were all together. We knew our mom and dad would be home in the evenings. We felt secure and stable, knowing we could depend on them and they would take good care of us.

Although we were a one-income household, we didn't seem to be without anything. My mom cooked every night, and we took vacations every summer. Our parents enjoyed dancing together, and they loved to jitterbug. They'd kiss each other hello and goodbye and would hug and kiss us goodnight. We were just like lots of families across the world. Nothing extraordinary.

Our family of four grew to include sons-in-law and grandchildren. We all held to the surety that cool-weather family gatherings included gumbo and potato salad. Dad, Doug, my husband, and Neil, my sister's husband, would be hunting from the first weekend in November until January. Thanksgiving and Christmas both included turkey and dressing, and at least one of those occasions would take place at my house. Daddy would be in his office working on tax returns from the beginning of March until mid-April. He would also be out in his rose garden several times a week. Twice a year when they were in bloom, he would share his beautiful Double Delight roses with the ladies at Subway, the grocery store, and me and Julie. Life was as predictable as his daily breakfast of two pancakes, two sausage patties, and one free senior coffee. Nothing extraordinary. Just life.

We had no idea he had entered the first stage of a long, seven-stage battle for his life. And his life was our lives. We did life together. Our hearts were, and still are, woven together. When one of us was knocked down, the rest of us carried him.

―――――

Daddy was a Certified Public Accountant. He was smart. He loved doing research, and he enjoyed working in the yard and growing roses. He loved being outside, hunting and fishing and playing golf. He drove a truck and listened to oldies rock-n-roll. He was an ordinary, typical, working man. He loved our mom, and he loved us.

There were no warning signs. No one in our family had suffered from Alzheimer's disease. His mom died young from heart trouble, but his dad lived to be 93 years old and sharp as your best knife. Nothing in our world indicated that he would be the next victim of this terrible aggressor.

Alzheimer's disease started its damage while he was working, driving, playing golf, hunting, growing roses, and living life. He had no idea, nor did we. It was a silent intruder that hid from us for an unknown number of years. What could have caused it to start? No one really knows. Was it sugar? Was it smoking? Was it depression? Was it a head injury or trauma? (He was a boxer when he was a kid.) No one knows. That's the scary part. No one knows how to prevent it or how to cure it. We were not prepared for what was to come. We were walking through life oblivious to what was hiding under the surface.

My dad lost one of his brothers in a one-car accident. His brother wouldn't have died if he had worn his seatbelt. The driver survived, but my uncle was thrown from the vehicle. When I started driving, my dad always told me to buckle-up. It wasn't a law back then, and I was way too cool, or so I thought. He would see me pull out of the driveway without putting on my seatbelt and he would follow me wherever I was headed. I'd arrive at my destination, get out of the car, and promptly get in trouble. I remember how angry he would be. He'd tell me in graphic detail the image of his brother lying in the hospital with the fatal head injury. As a young kid, I didn't grasp the fear he must have felt watching Julie and I drive off without our seatbelts fastened. He wanted us to be safe. As an adult, I understood his concern for me. As he moved through his disease, I had a fear of what was happening to him. I wanted him to be safe. I felt as helpless as he must have felt watching his brother die.

Ronnie Carlin experienced a horror no one would ever choose. His world was shrinking and closing in on him. He fought hard at first, refusing to acknowledge the strength of his opponent. When he realized Alzheimer's was bigger and stronger than he was, he armed himself with knowledge, so he could fight smarter and maybe win the round. He swung hard and landed a few punches with the help of medications he had been prescribed. However, he kept getting knocked down. After seven long rounds, he lost by TKO. He stayed in the ring and did his best to bob and weave. But Alzheimer's was just too much for him to overcome. Layer by layer his life was cruelly stripped away.

Chapter Four

<u>The Stages Of Grief</u>

As the loved ones of a person living with Alzheimer's, we suffer through the disease, each in our own way. For each stage of Alzheimer's our parent or loved one begins, we go through the stages of grief. The first couple of stages are vague, but grief hits you hard when you realize the battle has started. We mourn over and over as they disappear little by little.

It's such a strange thing to mourn a living person.

Shock and Denial come first. I would always ignore or deny it in the beginning. I would either explain it away or pretend it was no big deal. For me, the most prolonged period of shock and denial came during the second stage of Alzheimer's. When the symptoms were mild and few, it was easy to blame outside circumstances. His hearing loss was my go-to issue to use as an excuse for something he did that was out of character. *"Oh, he just didn't understand what you said."*

When the truth became undeniable, Pain and Guilt would take over. I'd cry and sink into a dark sadness. The brokenness inside would be too heavy to bear at times. Progression to a new stage was gradual but then would seem to appear from out of nowhere. As I would think about where we were, I'd feel guilty for not noticing the subtle symptoms of decline to this newest reality.

Anger and Bargaining did not last for long. I could be mad that he was sick, but that didn't make him better. I wasn't going to be angry at God, because He is sovereign and loved Daddy more than I could have imagined. I prayed for healing sometimes. I didn't doubt God could heal him. But honestly, I didn't think that was His plan through all of this. I mainly prayed for grace and mercy for my Dad. I prayed that people would be kind to him and that he wouldn't be afraid. I prayed he'd die before he forgot me. I know that sounds terribly selfish, and I guess it is. I knew his quality of life was diminishing and if he were at the point of not knowing his loved ones, his life would no longer be his own. I know so many of you reading this have experienced your loved one forgetting who you are. I can't imagine that feeling although I prepared myself mentally for it to happen. I'm just so thankful he died before he forgot me.

Depression, Reflection and Loneliness are next. This stage was a strong one for me, because I tend to become depressed and reflective quite easily when sadness comes. Part of the reason I started writing down things that were happening was to help me through the depression by reflecting on what was in the past and what was happening in the present. As I found it harder and harder to remember what he was like before Alzheimer's, the more I tried to write down things that were happening, so I didn't entirely forget. This stage of grief is very lonely. Depression causes you to withdraw from others. You are convinced no one wants to hear you whine about your situation. My mom would say that sometimes. She would tell me some bad things going on with Daddy and then say, *"I'm sorry. I know no one wants to hear me complain."* I've learned it's okay to talk about what you are going through. It's most beneficial if you are talking to a support group or someone who can empathize because they have been in your shoes. Not everyone understands the grief involved in watching a parent or loved one slowly lose their mind and to see them become someone who is a mere shell of the person you loved for your entire life.

The Upward Turn portion of grief was more of "*I'm tired of fighting it*" resolve for me. Things never got better, just easier to deal with.

The Reconstruction & Working Through stage is when you adapt your life to accommodate his. Small tweaks to your life make his more comfortable.

"*Hey, let's try on this really nice pair of slip-on sneakers. They look really good with your shorts.*"

You leave out the part about how much easier they will be to put on, now that he can't tie his own shoes.

You Accept and Hope. The new phase of Alzheimer's becomes your new reality. It is now your everyday way of life. You hope your loved one never gets worse, although you are just starting back at Stage One: Denial.

My dad's brother, Wayne, and his wife, Sandra came in from out of town for a visit. The three of us met Mom and Dad at the church so that my aunt and uncle could see the newly remodeled sanctuary and prayer room. Mom had not told Daddy that Wayne, Sandra, and I would be meeting them there. When Dad saw Wayne and Sandra, he was happy to see them, but not surprised. He didn't process that they lived a few hours away and their being at the church was out of the ordinary. Daddy and Wayne talked about the church and the beautiful replica of the Ark of the Covenant in the prayer room. Wayne told Daddy about the Ark and Moses and the Ten Commandments, and my dad listened as if it were the first time he had ever heard the stories. He loved hearing all about it, although it was something he once knew very well.

When it was time to go back to the house, we all said our goodbyes and headed to the parking lot. My uncle broke down crying first, then my aunt. They moved from Denial and entered Grief. I was a little dumbfounded. *"What's the deal? You knew he was sick,"* I said in my mind.

Sandra said, "Oh, Denise! We had no idea how far he had slipped."

"But you've talked to him on the phone. You couldn't tell?"

Wayne said, "He couldn't hear good on the phone, so I assumed that was what was wrong with him."

Sandra added, "You just don't understand. We remember him how he was."

"Well, I don't remember how he was. I know him as he is," I replied.

I wasn't rude or sarcastic. In my heart, I wished I could remember. I had accepted where he was. I had no other choice. His reality, and therefore ours, had changed drastically.

As the stages of Alzheimer's progressed, the time between them became shorter. Daddy seemed to slip quicker every step of the way. It was like a ball gaining momentum, rolling down a hill. The full grieving process had to speed up to keep up with the disease. Unfortunately, by the end of his life, I was getting pretty good at the stages of grief. They had become a part of my daily life just as Alzheimer's had become a part of his.

Chapter 5

Why Did I Write This Book?

I've tried to learn to deal with Alzheimer's on my own. I hated hearing people's stories about how it's going to get worse. Frankly, I really didn't want to know. I'd rather be blissfully ignorant until something new happened. I knew it was going to get worse, but I didn't want the specifics. As a matter of fact, I didn't go to Lamaze class when I had my daughter. The baby was coming out without me knowing all the gory details, and I was just fine with that.

I have a friend from church who gave me an invaluable piece of advice. One Sunday, after services, she and I talked out in the parking lot. My Dad had just been diagnosed, and I was searching to make some sense of what was happening. Gail had lost her father to Alzheimer's. She saw her mom struggle with denial, and she knew how it felt, as a daughter, to see her father stolen by this disease, right before her eyes.

"Start writing things down. There will be some good things and some bad things. Some things will also be funny. But, eventually, the funny things will stop. You need to write everything down, so you don't forget."

That was the first and only time someone gave me a hopeful direction in which to take this journey. I needed hope. I knew the disease, and I knew that what was going to happen to my Daddy and my family was not going to be good. However, I knew God can bring about good, even from bad things.

So why did I write this book? Because I really do wish I would have known what to expect. One thing I learned from reading books, articles, blogs, and Facebook group posts, is that every journey through Alzheimer's is different. The path is as unique as the person it affects. I wanted to share some of the things we learned and used to make Daddy's life and our lives less stressful during this time. Also, some things we tried weren't as helpful. My mom, my sister, and I learned how to best accommodate my Dad's ever-mounting difficulties with his thought processes and his physical changes. We attended a support group once or twice, but not on a regular basis. In hindsight, we should have been more diligent for our own mental health. We learned some calming techniques to use when Daddy was anxious or agitated. Julie was the best. She would make him look her in the eyes, and she would talk to him calmly. She'd also hold his hand or pat his leg. You could see his entire body physically relax. His face would soften, and his jaw unclench. She'd say, *"Do you trust me?"* He'd always say, *"Yes."* Except one time he said *"No."* She laughed because it wasn't that he didn't trust her. He just didn't want to do what she was telling him to do. It was beautiful to watch Daddy and Julie interact. They had such a tight bond and trust between them.

I also wanted to share things I journaled about Daddy's stages through this disease, as Gail suggested. Sometimes I would think he was experiencing something different from anyone else, then I'd read about it happening to lots of other patients. The caretakers were reaching out to the masses because they thought they were the only ones dealing with an issue. They would find they were not alone.

No one wants to be the only one. There is strength in numbers. There is comfort in numbers. People find themselves in someone else's details. Being able to relate to someone who is on the same battlefield can give us weapons of hope to keep fighting. It also gives us tidbits of wisdom needed to make the best decisions for the people we love.

I'm saying to others, *"I get it. You're right. This is awful. Have you tried this?"*

I'm hoping you will benefit from some of our lessons. I'm also hoping you feel a kinship with our family. Three of us survived and miss the head of our family terribly. We've been where you are and where you may be going.

Lastly, I wrote this book so Ronald M. Carlin will never be forgotten. I know I'll always remember him. However, some people will only remember him as impaired. I hate that most of all. He deserves better. I'm still grasping at vague memories of the father who raised me. The disease has stolen my memories of him, much in the cruel way it took his mind. When I think of conversations he and I would have, I have a hard time remembering him fully understanding and hearing me. I know he did. But, the recent past clouds my mind. I'm hoping to recover some of those good memories.

Alzheimer's disease was Ronnie Carlin's battle. It was not who He Was. He was so much more.

Chapter 6

Did We Miss Something?

It's hard to tell when Alzheimer's entered our lives. Stage One of Alzheimer's disease is the most mysterious. Daddy had no complaints of memory issues, and there were no memory problems detectable by his friends or by us. He was still mentally and physically active. His brain was still strong enough to hide the truth from all of us at this point. But somewhere in my dad's skull, defective proteins were beginning to build-up and harden, disrupting the normal functioning of his brain. It wasn't a normal aging process, but one that would slowly choke and shrink his brain into one that no longer was able to function correctly.

As I think back, I can identify a couple of instances that happened when he was in the second stage of the disease. He would have been in a very mild decline. What seemed to pounce on us out of the blue was really a slow process, beginning to reveal itself. Should we have known something was wrong at the time? In hindsight, everything is clear, but in real-time there are so many explanations for why someone does what they do.

HE WAS

My mom and dad loved to take vacations. They had been all over the United States, Canada, Europe, and Israel. They started traveling shortly after my sister married and we were both out of the house, going on guided trips so they wouldn't miss any landmarks or adventures. They would come home with foreign coins for the grandkids, small gifts for us, and lots of pictures. Every trip included a picture of Daddy eating ice cream in a famous city and a picture of a UPS truck for my now-retired UPS delivery-driver husband. They enjoyed their travels and saw so many beautiful things.

In 2009, they went on an overseas trip that began with a flight out of George Bush Intercontinental Airport in Houston, Texas. As was their routine, they would drive themselves to a hotel near the airport, spend the night and get up early to catch the international flight. I was at work the afternoon my mom called to say they had returned from their trip, retrieved the car and just left the airport to head home.

About 45 minutes later, Mom called my cell phone and was very upset. She told me that Daddy was driving down Loop 610 in Houston headed to IH-10 to come home. A lady behind them clipped the back of their car when she passed them, causing him to hit the concrete barrier on the highway with the driver's side of the vehicle. The impact blew out the two tires on that side of the car. They swerved and were able to cross several lanes of traffic to take the exit ramp and pull to safety on the feeder road. She was telling me about what happened, obviously shaken up and fussing about the lady who didn't seem to notice she had caused an accident. Daddy was standing outside of the car, looking at the damage.

Mom said, "Some man just pulled up and is talking to your Daddy." We kept talking, and then suddenly she started screaming,

"Oh my God! Your Daddy just got in the man's car, and they drove away!"

She was hysterical. Rightly so. Daddy didn't say where he was going, and mom didn't know who the man was. She was crying.

"He just left me here. I don't know where he went!"

I tried to calm her down, but I was upset, too. What was he thinking? He may have just been kidnapped. We had no idea. He didn't have a cell phone, and we had no way of finding him. They weren't in the best part of town, and it was starting to get dark.

Using my office phone, I called the Houston Police Department and told them where the car was and what had happened. I also called the road-side service and gave them the same information. It was terrible. I couldn't wrap my mind around his thought process. My mom was still panic-stricken and inconsolable. It was so dangerous for him to get in a stranger's car. Did he not think mom would need to know he was going somewhere? What was he thinking? That's all I could say.

After 20 excruciatingly long minutes, the police arrived. Shortly after that, my dad and the man came back. It turns out that the man had a tire shop around the corner from where they had parked. He and my Dad rode to his shop to see if he had tires to replace the ones that were torn up, which he did not. A wrecker was called, and the driver took my parents to the dealership where he was towing the car for repair. Since it was now late in the evening, the dealership was closed, and the car wouldn't be repaired until the next day. My parents needed a ride home. I called a co-worker from our Houston office to pick them up at the dealership and drop them off at a restaurant on the highway. Doug and I picked them up there.

It had been a rough afternoon. Daddy saw no reason that mom would have been so upset. She was still furious at him, but grateful he was safe.

It was such a strange incident and very uncharacteristic of my Dad. He has always been so responsible and protective of my Mom. Leaving her on the side of the highway without any explanation was abnormal. At the time, I figured he was shaken up by the accident and was trying to fix the situation. Looking back, I'm not sure if that was a valid excuse or not.

The following year, they took another overseas trip. On their way home from the same airport, Daddy took a wrong turn and got lost. He had made this trip many times before without incident. However, on this day, it took them three hours to get home when it would typically take them an hour and a half. Again, we thought he was daydreaming or something. One goof-up in a year does not constitute an all-out intervention. It's easily explained away. I really think he had entered the second stage of Alzheimer's disease. He was overall normal in every way, but the progress of the beta-amyloid plaques were starting to cause misfires in his brain. It was short-circuiting his cognitive reasoning and manifesting itself in lapses of judgment. He was 67 years old.

Chapter 7

Paradise In Sour Lake

My Dad owned 97 acres of heaven in Sour Lake, Texas. It originally belonged to my mom's step-father, Nicky Debes' family. Daddy hunted there for years with my step-grandfather, PawPaw, as we called him. He began researching the undivided interest in the land and found there were several owners. Some had passed away, and some lived in Syria, where the family had immigrated from in the late 1800s. He spent years contacting the owners or their surviving heirs and working out a purchase of their portion. Eventually, he was able to buy all the land, with the exception of one acre. He secured an easement for the entrance because there was no road leading onto the property. He dug a pond, built a campsite, and made it his own heaven on earth. He called it the "Carlin Killin' Time Ranch" and hung a sign with the name at the front gate. He was so proud of what he had built.

He loved every inch of this land, and he knew it well. He could tell you about the trees and which ones he had hunted near and which ones fell over during past storms. He'd talk about the first and second prairies, which were clearings in the trees. There were several deer stands and lots of shooting lanes. He also had four dynamite holes. They were the result of past searches for oil on the property when people would blast holes as part of their seismic testing. Now they are full of water. The wild hogs loved the brush and mud surrounding them. He and I even found a catfish in one of them.

He was his most content and happy standing on the levee of his pond. He had this pond dug many years ago. They dug a massive trench in an oval shape, throwing the dirt up on the sides to form a dam. As the rain filled the pond, it filled the ditch and eventually covered most of the center. The levee was kept mowed so he could walk around the edges and fly fish for the perch and bass he purchased to stock the pond. In the middle, he had two wood duck boxes. He joined a program with a department of the state that was studying the wood ducks, and he got nesting boxes from them. He LOVED the wood ducks. He'd get in his little aluminum boat and row out to check on them every weekend. He wasn't the only thing that loved the wood ducks. Unfortunately, so did snakes. They ate the eggs. Daddy built all kinds of homemade contraptions to stop the snakes from getting into the boxes. I remember going out there with him and seeing a snake skeleton intertwined in the chicken-wire guard below the box. It was creepy, but he was thrilled he had saved the ducks.

Daddy took his movie camera out to the woods and made videos. They were so funny to watch. Funny wasn't his intention, but he was not a very good filmmaker. He would narrate his adventures in a slow, monotone voice.

"Today is Saturday, May 3rd. It's a little breezy. We're here at the pond on this beautiful morning. This is the south side of the pond. (*Slow pan to the left*). This is the north side of the pond. (*Slow pan to the right*). The south side. (*Slow pan back to the left*). The north side. (*Slow pan back to the right*)."

He'd get excited if he caught a glimpse of a fish or deer or wood duck. The slow, calm narration became fast and loud as he laughed and pointed out the creature. We had a 30-minute video of him riding his four-wheeler at two miles-per-hour around his property while he described the landscape. The only problem was that he had hung the camera by the wrist strap on the handlebar of the ATV, so the entire video was upside down.

My favorite video was of him narrating his day as he floated up to a wood duck box in the pond. He told about the momma duck he had seen the previous week and how he hoped to find some eggs. He said he didn't want to disturb her, so he was whispering and moving slowly. He leaned in with the camera, putting the lens up to the little entrance hole. Suddenly, he screams; there's a huge commotion, lots of *"Dern its"* and the camera was filming sky, water, and Daddy, as he dropped it into the boat. The scene went blank for just a second, and then everything went back into focus. He opened the door to the box, revealing a big chicken snake coiled up with three eggs protruding from within its body. He hated losing eggs to the snakes.

When I first moved back to town from Houston, I would go fishing and "fiddle-farting" with him quite a bit. I was lonely and needed something to do on those weekends when my daughter was with her dad. We always enjoyed our time together. He seemed different out there. In everyday life, he was like the rest of us. Get up, go to work, stay busy, etcetera. But in his woods, his whole countenance changed. He moved slower. He looked at each tree. He pointed out little animals and bugs. He breathed deep as if to take it all in. He was at peace and calm. Sharing those moments with him was nice. Our trips to the woods were peaceful and relaxing and good for his soul. They were good for mine, too.

I went deer hunting with him a few times. I went because he asked, but I didn't really want to kill anything. I'll cook it, but I didn't want to shoot it. We spent many early mornings and late afternoons sitting and watching. In Southeast

HE WAS

Texas, it's still hot at the beginning of deer season. The only thing worse than the heat was the mosquitos. Even the attractive mosquito net I wore over my head and face didn't protect me from the buzzing and bites. It was pretty miserable. However, I did like sharing his bag of M&M's and whispering because we were bored.

One late evening, we were sitting up high in a box blind. A large buck stepped into sight. Daddy got excited and whispered, "Aim for his neck and pull the trigger slowly." I did both and "Boom" the gun went off. The deer jumped and ran off. Daddy's started saying, "You got him! We're going to sit here for a little bit to be sure he's dead." I didn't know if I hit him or not. I somewhat hoped I hadn't. We waited about five minutes, and then we went looking for a blood trail. We never found one, so I'm pretty sure I missed. Daddy was convinced I shot the deer, but it had run off into the brush. The deer grew bigger every time he proudly told the story about the one that got away.

When I married Doug, I stopped going out there with Daddy. I'm not sure why, but I wasn't lonely anymore, and Doug loved going with him. They developed their relationship out in those woods. Both Doug and my brother-in-law, Neil, spent many weekends and hunting seasons with him. Lots of deer and hogs were killed in those woods. Lots of steaks were cooked at the camp. It was a place full of happy memories. But over the years, my dad went from being very particular about his land to being difficult. He also became dangerous.

One of the very first and disturbing incidents that screamed Alzheimer's took place in those woods.

My dad and Neil were working to get ready for hunting season. Usually, my husband would be there, too, but we were remodeling our house, and he was at home waiting for the contractor. Neil was on a tractor mowing trails and shooting lanes. He mowed through some brush and stirred up a hornet's nest. Immediately, he was swarmed and covered in hornets. They stung him all over his head, face, and hands. He jumped off the tractor and ran back to the camp, dropping his cell phone along the way.

When he got to the camp where Daddy was working, he frantically told him what happened. My dad didn't understand what he was saying. At the time I blamed the hearing loss and faulty hearing aids. Neil told Dad to take him to the hospital. Daddy never seemed to understand. Instead of realizing the severity of what was transpiring, he handed Neil the keys to his truck so he could drive himself. Neil ended up using Dad's cell phone, calling my sister to say he was on his way home. Neil was okay in the end, but it could have turned out so much worse.

My sister called me while Neil was headed home and told me what happened. Doug was going to have to go get Daddy since Neil left him in the woods without his truck.

I called Daddy on his cell phone.

"Hello."

"Daddy! Why didn't you take Neil to the hospital?"

"What?"

"Neil was stung by a swarm of hornets. He could have died. Did you not realize what happened?"

"Who?"

"Neil! He just left the woods because he was stung. Do you not understand what's happening?"

"Oh yeah. Neil got stung. I'm having a root beer. Sure is good. We've been working hard out here."

"Daddy! Julie called me and said Neil is coming home covered in hornet stings. Why didn't you drive him?"

"Julie? Your sister, Julie? Oh sure. I saw her this morning. She made us some turkey sandwiches with mayonnaise. They were good, good."

"Stop talking about sandwiches. Listen to me. Neil was hurt. I am trying to figure out why you didn't help him."

"...and chocolate cookies. Super good! Super! And turkey sandwiches."

"Stop! Listen to me. Did you know Neil was hurt? He was stung by a swarm of hornets."

"Yeah. Neil got stung by a hornet. I gave him my keys, and he went home. Did I tell you Julie made some chocolate cookies? They were super good!"

This conversation went on for a while. Neil was okay and ended up going back out there to get his phone and my dad. Daddy remained oblivious to the gravity of the situation. All he talked about was the cookies.

That was a symptom of Alzheimer's called "Inappropriate affect." Inappropriate affect is defined as displaying emotion, behavior, and/or demeanor that is not appropriate for the event, situation, or thought that is occurring or being expressed. Smiling when giving someone bad news is an example of inappropriate affect. Inappropriate affect, like other affect disorders, can be symptoms of dementia and Alzheimer's disease.[6]

What is so evident in hindsight was bewildering at the time. He couldn't hear well, and you had to repeat yourself several times. That part of the conversation was normal. His reaction was not. I chalked it up to not hearing what I was saying. I was as oblivious as he was at the time, just to the other truth swarming around us that day. Doug, Neil, and Julie knew something was wrong.

This took place in 2012. Daddy was still working and driving. But it was the earliest, most prominent memory I have of there being no denying something was wrong. But I was in denial at the time. I didn't know what was going on in his head. I was looking for a rational explanation for an irrational situation, rather than seeing the truth.

A short time later, Doug and Daddy were walking down a path through the woods where they had been hunting. Doug was walking in front of my Dad when Dad's rifle went off, shooting the trail to the side of Doug. Doug screamed, "What happened?" Daddy responded, "Nothing. I was just checking to see if there was a bullet in the chamber."

Doug was mad and scared of what Daddy could be capable of doing. Not maliciously, but carelessly. Safety, especially gun safety, had been a top priority for my Dad and a strict rule out in his woods. He knew better than to pull the trigger. But he did. Why? What was he thinking?

A similar incident happened with my brother-in-law, Neil. That time my dad shot straight up in the air, checking for a bullet in the chamber.

Doug and Neil were afraid to be out in the woods with him if he had a gun. They were concerned about his safety. Not only could he shoot them, but he could shoot himself. He had started shuffling and stumbling. He could fall and get hurt, and they would not know where to find him. Daddy once knew every inch of his land. Every tree, every bush, every marker. He got lost and panicked that deer season. The guys could not deny the obvious.

Before you say, "Then why didn't you take away his gun?" think about all the dynamics at play. He was the authority figure in the scenario. He was the landowner and the father-in-law. Mentally he was capable of many things, and he had not been formally diagnosed. We had not concluded that he needed to see a doctor or that anything was wrong with him. He was still teaching accounting, and driving. The two incidents of him discharging his gun to clear the chamber were not something that had been happening. It was a new development. New and seemingly isolated. We just knew something wasn't right.

Chapter 8

And On Stage #3, We Have Reality

Daddy was driving and teaching school and living life as usual, but things had begun to change. He kept having "someone" run into him in parking lots and damaging his truck. The first two times were at his hearing doctor's office building. Both times there was a massive dent in the passenger's side of the truck. It was unthinkable that someone would do that much damage and leave the scene. He had the first dent repaired and almost immediately, it happened again. The third time it happened, all of us, except Mom, realized he was the one hitting the car next to him. A visit from the local constable's office, serving him with a summons to small claims court, confirmed our suspicion. A gentleman witnessed Daddy pulling into a parking space at the hearing doctor's office building. He turned too sharply, hitting the back bumper of the neighboring car with the back fender well of his truck. He didn't feel the impact or hear the crunching of the metal as the two cars crashed together. Dad got out of his truck and went into the building. The witness stayed and waited on the owner of the damaged car to return. He had written down Daddy's license plate number and told her what happened. She left after getting the information. Daddy walked out, and the witness told him that he had seen him hit the other car. Dad was angry.

He told the man he was wrong, and the other person hit his truck. He was hot when he got home. He told Mom about this person hitting him in the parking lot and then saying it was his fault. Mother told me the story, and then I talked to Daddy. His story didn't make sense. He said the car was gone and that the guy must have moved it somewhere else. He was convinced the man claiming to be the witness was, in fact, the person who hit his truck and was trying to get something over on him. I told my Mom I thought Daddy was the one causing the wrecks, because what are the odds of his truck getting hit three different times, in the same place, within such a short period of time. She bowed up and said, "Why on earth would you accuse your father of lying? Of course, he would know if he hit someone else's vehicle. You have no idea what you are talking about!" Although she was the closest to him, she didn't see it. Maybe because she was the nearest to him, she didn't want to see it.

Mom, Julie, and I went to the Justice of the Peace court with Daddy. He was visibly nervous. We stood close to him, and all prayed together before court began. The lady who sued him kept staring at him with a mean look. It made me mad because I knew he was having problems and he was upset. The lady took the stand and told her story. Her witness also told his story. Then my Dad had his chance. He said they were all lying, he didn't know why, but they were. He also answered the attorney's questions with several *"Huh?"* and *"What did you say?"* He was confused and looked like someone with Alzheimer's disease. It was an awful thing to witness. In the end, he lost the case, and his insurance had to pay. Although there was no denying he was impaired, I rejected it anyway. I was not ready to admit to the truth. Not yet.

HE WAS

When Daddy retired from the energy company and his CPA practice, he began to teach accounting at a local state college. He loved teaching students, and they loved him. Dad had been an average student in college, trying to finish school and start a family. I think he had some ADHD, so reading and understanding what he read the first time, the second time, or even third time must have been difficult for him. Actually, I know he had ADHD. If you stood next to him for more than two minutes, you knew. He was a fidgeter.

Despite his inability to sit still, he was a great teacher. He didn't have much money when he was in school, so he didn't want kids to spend too much money on books. He really wanted them to learn and love accounting like he did. When I went back to college as an adult, I started with a second-semester accounting class. I asked the kids sitting around me who they had for the first semester, and they would tell me, "Mr. Carlin at the Port Arthur campus." They then started talking about how he was the best, and everyone made an "A" in his class. He was super easy and super nice, they said. Students had his home number, and they knew they could call him anytime, and he would walk them through the homework assignment. He won "Teacher of the Year" a couple of times and students invited him to their awards ceremonies and graduations. He loved to read the student's critiques from the end of the semester surveys because they liked him. They would say such wonderful things about how much he helped them and how much he cared. It gave him a sense of accomplishment and pride.

He had a rough time after being let go when the company he had been with for so many years was bought out by a bigger corporation. He was too young to retire, so they put him, a CPA, in an entry-level data-entry clerk position. A few weeks into the job, they said he had a bad attitude. He told them what to do with their opinion and quit. He had worked so hard for that company and loved what he did.

The transition took a heavy toll on him. He slept a lot and stayed in his chair watching TV most days. He didn't seem to have much will to do much of anything. He was depressed.

After some months, he decided to open his own CPA practice, sharing an office with another CPA with whom he had worked for many years. He wasn't a salesperson, so he wasn't one to go out and drum up business. Also, because of the depression, he laid in his chair and didn't bring in many new clients. I know he was praying for a break-through and guidance from God about what he should do next.

The job at the college was the answer to his prayers. It gave him dignity and pride in a job well done. He was a good teacher, too. I helped him set up spreadsheets as grade sheets, and we worked together to get his lesson plans and tests formatted. He enjoyed every minute of his time there. The kids didn't usually get his Sanford & Son references, and they thought it was funny that he talked to his thumb when they all sat silently when he asked them a question. But, they knew he cared about them. They knew he wanted them to succeed.

In 2010, Dad decided to retire after being with the college for ten years. His hearing had worsened over the years, and we figured that was causing some issues in school. Also, I had to help him more with the spreadsheets and the lesson plans and tests. He seemed to be messing them up and not being able to fix them. That was something new. Until soon before he retired, he was able to work his word processing and spreadsheet programs with ease. He only called me when he had a particularly tricky issue.

Julie and I threw him a surprise retirement party. We invited all his friends, and there was a good crowd. I was standing near the entrance with Daddy when he introduced himself to a gentleman he had known for many years from his Sunday School class. The man said, "I know who you are, and you know who I am. That's why I'm here." Daddy said, "Okay. Good. Thanks for coming." It was weird and very out of character. It was awkward, too. It was apparent he had forgotten someone he should have known.

When his replacement at the college suddenly became ill, the school asked my dad to come back. He worked for three more years. Those were three long years. He started getting bad reviews from the students. They would say he mumbled. And, I had to help him with his documents and spreadsheets almost daily. His students were now the age of my kids or a little older. I was told by one of his students I knew, that he was "a sweet little PawPaw," but they learned nothing in his class because he made no sense. They laughed at him telling stories and how some people ignored him. He went from someone who had been respected to someone people laughed at. How horrible! He didn't deserve to be laughed at or disrespected.

How do you tell your father that he has a problem? I couldn't.

Unfortunately, society told him. And he didn't believe it.

In 2013, my mom took a trip with her life-long best friend to Israel. I was in charge of making sure Daddy was entertained and fed. After dinner one night, he asked me to come over and fold the towels he had washed. He said he didn't remember how to fold them the way mom did them. I went there and helped him. He seemed a little confused, nervous, and uncomfortable. A few nights later, he showed up at my house in the early evening. He pulled up a chair in the kitchen as I was cooking dinner. I could tell something was wrong. He said his boss told him he wasn't doing a good job and he would not be returning the next semester. He was heartbroken. He was sad, and he was defeated. He told me he didn't understand why his boss was saying these things and he couldn't imagine who was complaining about him. He said it like he was trying to figure out if his boss was right, rather than in a defiant way. It was like he realized he wasn't functioning 100%, but he couldn't put his finger on what was happening to him. It broke my heart. I tried to make him feel better and tell him how great retirement would be. But there was nothing I could say to make any of this better. I didn't want to admit the things people were saying were right, but I knew they were. I was just so angry at his boss for telling him. If no one says anything, then it's not true … right? I hated that he had to go home alone that night. I knew his world was crashing down around him.

Chapter 9

No More Denying

Moving through the days at the beginning of his battle, we saw some things, now looking back in hindsight, that should have been glaring tell-tale signs, like the getting lost, and the incidents in the woods. However, there's this awkward time when that person is still very lucid in their mind but having some issues. How do you approach him and say, *"Daddy you're 85% okay, and 15% not. We need to get you some help."* It's complicated, confusing, and it stinks. When the car accidents began, and he lost his job, we needed to get real with ourselves and real with him.

People always ask me if he started repeating things. I guess that's what most people think about Alzheimer's disease and how it can be recognized in their loved one. We did notice there were some strange things he had started saying and repeating. It was hard to detect if he was retelling stories because of the disease or because he was having fun. He has always told stories and "Boudreaux and Thibodeaux" jokes. He loved to talk and to be social, and he loved to tell funny stories repeatedly. He would start laughing hard right before the punch line. He cracked himself up.

The things we noticed as out of the ordinary were things like his obsession with numbers. He's always been a numbers guy. However, on birthdays he started saying things like, "Your momma is 40 for the 28th time;" or "You're 21 for the 25th time." He stopped saying how old someone was. Even when it wasn't a birthday. He described age as a significant age plus the number of years since then. He did that until we had to finally ask him to stop because he would repeat it over and over. Funny thing was, his math was right most of the time. The only age he would say was, "My Daddy was 93 years old when he died. Ninety-three! I am going to live to be 93." He was really obsessed about being 93 when he died.

He also started talking gibberish. He would be in the middle of a sentence and start making this "blah, blah, blah" sound like a baby does with their tongue before they can speak. When he first started this, it was annoying. We thought he was silly, and it wasn't funny. He'd make this sound and wiggle his fingers under his chin. We couldn't figure out why he would do that. I told Julie I thought he was repeating what he heard us say and because his hearing was so bad, it sounded like gibberish. That's a good explanation. Right? I was always looking for excuses. I couldn't blame his hearing when he started imitating people's mannerisms when they were speaking to him. He would stare at them with a little grin on his face and start moving his hands around like they did when they talked. It was embarrassing when we didn't know the person. He did this to my mom quite a bit because she is very animated in the way she talks. He would sometimes do it in front of her, and she would fuss at him. Most of the time he would stand behind her and move his hands and arms around, moving his mouth like he was talking, just like her. It was funny. It was like watching a kid misbehave.

Sometimes things he'd say were funny, and then I'd stop and realize they weren't funny. It would be funny if he said it on purpose, but he was serious. I would be in disbelief when I listened to him talk or try to explain something to me or ask me a question. He wasn't trying to be funny. He was trying to communicate. His blessings at the dinner table became conversations with God about what was going on that day and ended with "talk with you later" instead of "amen." We'd all say, "And God bless the food" because he would leave that part out. It was funny at first. It became bittersweet later, listening to him talk to God as his friend.

Too many things were now manifesting in his daily life. I couldn't explain away the new quirks and misunderstandings any longer. He wasn't just getting old. Something was happening to him. It seemed he had gone from a little "off" to almost child-like confusion. It was an undeniable slip from slightly and mildly diminished to noticeably and moderately impaired. It seemed to happen quickly. Either that or I finally opened my eyes and saw the truth.

Chapter 10

I've Seen This Before

Daddy's brain was damaged before we knew anything was wrong. He would get very emotional at times. He would tear-up and almost cry when he was proud, or he was happy, or sad, or excited. Any strong emotion caused him to tear up and start to cry a little. It was uncomfortable and concerning at first. I then realized I had experienced this type of emotional reaction from three other people in the past.

It is called Pseudobulbar Affect (PBA). It's a condition that's characterized by episodes of sudden uncontrollable and inappropriate laughing or crying. Crying appears to be a more common sign of PBA than laughing. It typically occurs in people with neurological conditions or injuries, including stroke, amyotrophic lateral sclerosis (ALS), multiple sclerosis (MS), traumatic brain injury, Alzheimer's disease, or Parkinson's disease.[7]

When I was in high school, I had a boyfriend named Gregg. His mom had a stroke a few years before we met. His mom, Dorothy, wasn't very verbal because her stroke damaged her speech. But she could tell you what she wanted by pointing and making a lot of grunting sounds. I was amazed at how well she could communicate. And she and Gregg's sister, Lori, were so fun to be around. They'd laugh and joke in a manner of communication they developed, using short words and hand motions.

On my way to meet Dorothy for the first time, Gregg told me about her condition and told me she cried a lot. It had something to do with the brain damage caused by the stroke and to not be alarmed. She wasn't sad. It was just something she did. When we arrived, he introduced us to each other. Dorothy smiled, then cried, then smiled and cried at the same time. I was 16 years old, and I really wasn't sure how to react. He had warned me, but it's not a situation you run into every day. Throughout our visit, I enjoyed watching them together. He would be silly to make her smile and laugh. They had a cute relationship. At the end of the day, we were sitting on the front porch swing. Gregg was in the middle. His mom and I were on either side of him with his arms around us both. He said, "What a wonderful day I've had being with my two favorite ladies." She started crying. I wanted to burst out and say, *"He's just kidding. You are his favorite. Please don't be sad."* I knew she wasn't sad. But I didn't know how to react. I knew it was hard on her, too. Being with her became much more comfortable with time, as I grew to know her and love her. She was a sweet lady who loved her kids.

A few years later, my sister, Julie, married Neil. Neil had been in a severe car accident and sustained a life-threatening head injury. He had brain damage and was still recovering when he and my sister started dating. Whenever he would get happy, sad, excited, or any strong emotion, he did the same thing Dorothy did. He would cry. It was hard on him. But as his brain healed, his symptoms lessened and went away.

I had the unfortunate opportunity to witness this a third time a few years later. My first husband's brother, Gary, had extremely high blood pressure, which resulted in him having a stroke at the age of 39. His stroke was debilitating and caused extreme paralysis on one side of his body. It affected his thought process, his speech, and his emotions. He started pointing and motioning and grunting to get his point across, just like Dorothy had done. I was able to quickly pick up on what he wanted because I had been through this before. Another recognizable side-effect emerged. His strong emotions came out as tears. I felt like the Lord had prepared me for Gary by putting Dorothy and Neil in my life. I knew the tears were a result of misfires in the brain. But it's hard to watch someone you love not be able to tell you what they want and what they need. They struggle for words and to maintain their composure, but the impairment resulting from brain damage takes over their emotions.

Daddy's symptoms of Pseudobulbar Affect were not as pronounced as Dorothy, Neil, or Gary's. He would start by telling you how proud of you or how much he loved you, and then he'd choke-up and tear-up. It wasn't sobbing crying. It was more of a soft cry. It was as if his heart was full and overflowing from his eyes. We wouldn't point out the tears. We'd just tell him it's okay.

And it was.

Chapter 11

The Talk

During the time my mom was on her trip to Israel and Daddy lost his job at the college, my sister and I had some serious conversations about what needed to happen. We both agreed he needed to see a doctor because he was having major cognitive issues. It was 2013. He was almost 70 years old.

Doug and I flew to Kansas City to see my in-laws on the same day my mom flew home from her trip to Israel. She called me when she got back to let me know she had made it safely and to check that we had arrived, too. I told her that we needed to talk about Daddy when I got home. My mom pushed the issue and wanted to know what I wanted to talk about, although I didn't think it was the time and I wanted to talk to her face-to-face, with my sister present. I told her that something was wrong with Daddy and we needed to address what was happening. She was a little perplexed and said she hadn't really noticed anything.

When I got home, Mom, Julie, Daddy, and I sat down in mom and dad's den to talk. We told our Dad that we had noticed he was having some difficulties. We were vague and didn't say, *"You are doing some crazy stuff."* We were trying to be gentle and respectful. He would smile at us, seeming somewhat confused, looking back and forth between Julie and me. It was as if he were trying to comprehend what we were saying. He said he was fine, and he hadn't noticed anything different about himself. Mom somewhat agreed with him. They looked at Julie and I as if we were speaking a foreign language, unsure of why we were bringing up this subject. Julie finally asked him, "Do you know we love you very much?"

"Sure. I love you both, too."

"Daddy, do you trust me?"

"Of course."

"If you trust me, then you know I only want what is best for you, and I want to help you if you need help."

"I don't think I need any help. Do you think I need help?"

"Yes. We both do. We are going to get you an appointment with a neurologist in Houston. The doctor can help you figure out what may be causing some of these issues you are having. He will be able to tell you what we can do to help you."

Daddy agreed to see a doctor, but only because he loved us. He didn't think he needed any help. Mom went along with our suggestion, but she did so out of trusting Julie's concern. Julie is her "medical" daughter. I'm the "accounting and fixing things" daughter.

Julie and I suspected Alzheimer's disease based on the symptoms we had been witnessing. I mentioned to a friend, who was the wife of my dad's Sunday School teacher, that we had noticed he was having some problems. She said she had seen some things with him, as well. She said once in bible class, the teacher said something about the prophet, Jeremiah. Daddy blurted out, "He was a bullfrog." He didn't laugh or anything like he was trying to be funny. Had he started singing the old Three Dog Night song, "Joy to the

World" about Jeremiah being a bullfrog, it would have been funny and made sense. But he didn't. He just said it and moved on. I mentioned to her that we were looking for an Alzheimer's doctor. A few days later she showed up at my front door with a booklet from the Nantz National Alzheimer Center at Methodist Hospital. They had been at the Methodist Hospital complex for something else and saw this advertisement booklet. We made an appointment and headed to Houston.

Chapter 12

The Truth

On the day of his first appointment, Daddy was dressed as sharp as usual. Every hair in place, clothes neat and pressed, shoes shined. He smelled good and looked great. But you could see some anxiety in his demeanor. We all were anxious. We had no idea what the day held in store for us, but we all felt the unease of what we would have to face.

This was not the first family trip we had taken together. Every summer of our childhood we took a vacation. Daddy would drive, mom would ride shot-gun, Julie and I sat in the back. The close proximity in the backseat led to many skirmishes between us sisters after way too many hours in the car. My mother split us up by putting Julie next to Daddy in the front seat, and she sat in the back with me. Julie loved being up front as the co-pilot.

The trip this day was different for many reasons. It wasn't a vacation. And for the first time, Julie was the driver and Daddy was the co-pilot. I could see his hand tapping nervously to the music coming out of the radio. He didn't say much, but he was antsy. I was in the backseat with Mom. She has this funny habit of reading every street sign, billboard, and storefront out loud and making commentary.

"Oh look, Bob's Flowers. Aren't those pretty?"

"Channelview 10 miles. We are getting close."

"Joe Myers Ford. That was my Paw Paw's name."

Julie told Daddy to watch for the police because she's a fast driver. She wanted to give him a job and purpose because she was aware of how emasculating it is to have your daughter drive you somewhere, instead of the other way around. She was also trying to get his mind off our plans for the day.

"Daddy. When you see a policeman, you need to say, 'Slow down. There's the Po Po.'"

He laughed. "What's the Po Po?"

"That's what the kids called the police these days."

We were cruising, quickly, down I-10 through the rice fields, when Julie saw a police car.

"Daddy! You are supposed to be looking out for me. There's a police car. You are supposed to say, 'There's the Po Po,' so I don't get pulled over." He laughed and said it.

A little farther down the highway, she sees another police car. "Daddy! You aren't doing a very good job of keeping me from getting a ticket. There's another Po Po."

He laughed, saying, "I'm sorry." He was having fun.

We pulled into the Medical Center, which is a massive area in Houston consisting of many hospitals and physician complexes. Daddy started pointing and saying excitedly, "Shug, slow down! There's the Hoo Pa Pa."

We all started laughing. Daddy was trying to help, but I guess the slang was too much to remember.

We went into the doctor's office and were immediately shown to a room. Daddy was fidgeting, as he did when he was nervous or anxious. Julie sat on one side of him, and Mom sat on the other. I sat next to Mom. It was suffocating in that room. At least it was for me. We didn't really talk amongst ourselves much. Just small talk and idle words to fill the tense air.

The doctor came in and introduced himself to us. He began by asking my dad some questions about his life, and whether or not he had noticed any changes in his thinking. He asked my Dad to tell him about us. Dad liked telling the doctor that he was a certified public accountant. He also shared with the doctor that he and my mother had been married for 50 years. He and the doctor continued to have a conversation. When he would trip up on words or hesitate during his explanation, my mom would answer for him or correct him with the right word. The doctor asked her to stop. He told her he needed to be able to evaluate Daddy. She looked surprised. I don't think she realized that she had been helping him so much. She and Daddy looked at each other somewhat sadly. It was an unspoken moment of fear for them both.

The doctor told my dad to remember three words – black, sock, and adore. He would say it a few times and have Daddy repeat it. Then he moved on to asking Mom, Julie, and me questions about why we felt he had some impairment. As Daddy looked at me with a trusting, small smile, I had to tell the doctor about his inability to do taxes *"as good as he had in the past."* He didn't stop smiling. It was like he didn't know how to react. We had to talk about his issues and short-comings in front of him. I was so uncomfortable, and my heart broke for him. I felt like I was being unfaithful to him. I wasn't honoring him in the way he deserved. It was so cruel for him to have to sit there and listen to us basically tell the doctor that he was losing his mind. Daddy didn't interrupt us, but he smiled sadly at each one of us. We were betraying him right in front of his face. It was horrible. I was so mad at the doctor for making us do this.

The doctor asked him to repeat the three things he was supposed to remember. "Black, sock, adore," Daddy said confidently as he stuck his foot out and pointed to his black sock.

The doctor continued asking Dad and us questions. Julie and I stepped out of the room for a few minutes so Mom and Dad could talk to the doctor about personal issues. When we came back in, the doctor asked him to repeat the three things again. With his foot out, he said, "black, sock." Then he paused, thinking intently. Again, he said, "black, sock." He turned and looked to mom for help. She told him the word. The doctor said, "Don't help him. I need to see how he remembers these things." Mom frowned at being corrected, and Daddy said, "I remember. It's black, sock, adore." I realized at that moment why we didn't truly know the severity of his impairment. He and mom were tag-teaming life. She was covering for him and just thought she was helpful. I guess that's expected when you've been married for a half-century. The doctor scheduled him for some testing; a CAT scan, MRI, psychological exam, among other things. He suspected Daddy had Parkinson's because his right hand trembled somewhat and his facial movements were limited when he talked. He had a stoic look on his face even when he said something funny. For some reason, I was relieved by the Parkinson's pre-diagnosis. I know it's a terminal, awful disease. I guess it was the hope that although his body would eventually betray him, his mind would not go as quickly.

We headed home, stopping for dinner before the end of our trip. It was a long day. It was the first of many, many long days. But we were getting closer to an answer.

Over the next few weeks, the MRI and CAT scan tests were completed, and he was scheduled to have a comprehensive psychological exam. During this test, he would spend four to five hours with a therapist while going through a series of memory and logic tests. Sometime between the medical tests and the psychological test, we were having a family dinner at a local Italian restaurant. Out of the blue, he looked at me, pointed his finger at me and said, "You said I couldn't do tax returns. I can do tax returns. Why did you say that?" It had been swimming around in his memory for weeks now. He felt the betrayal and finally confronted me.

"I didn't say you couldn't do them. I said they are becoming more difficult for you."

"No. You said I couldn't do taxes anymore." He was getting agitated.

"I'm so sorry, Daddy. I didn't mean to hurt your feelings. I told him tax returns were getting more difficult for you to do. He needs to know that, so he can help you. You've always been so great at doing tax returns. When you're off your game, it's noticeable to me. I love you, and I don't want to hurt your feelings."

I was so mad at the doctor for making us talk about him and say truthful, yet hurtful, things in front of his already grieving and fearful heart. It was so demeaning for him.

The four of us headed back to Houston for Daddy's psychological testing. The doctor spoke with us for a few minutes, again asking us to detail our dad's decline in front of him. It has something to do with HIPAA and a patient's right to know the information being given to the doctor. In this case, I felt his right to dignity trumped HIPAA. I hated being part of this questioning.

A woman named Wendy came into the room and introduced herself. She took him in the back and said he would be staying through lunch. Mom told her that lunch was very important to him, so they said they would get him a sandwich. Mom said, "With mustard, no vegetables." Dad chimed in, "And chips and a soda pop. Root beer. I like root beer." It was like he was being left with a sitter.

He was excited to spend the day answering questions. He saw it as a test that he was going to ace. The academic in him liked making a good grade. Mom, Julie and I went down to a restaurant in the building and ate lunch. We made small talk, but I kept thinking about him. He loved a captive audience and telling stories. Wendy seemed friendly, and I knew he would enjoy himself. I just hoped he wouldn't be overwhelmed or feel like he couldn't do what they were asking. He should be able to keep his dignity as a smart, capable, human being. Alzheimer's was trying to strip it away.

When he came out of testing, he was so excited.

"The lady I visited with ... her name was ... like the hamburger place ... the one with the red-headed girl ... Wendy!"

That was cognitive reasoning stepping in to help where his memory had faded. He told us all about the tests and said he had passed them all. He was proud that he had done an excellent job.

A few weeks later, we reconvened at the doctor's office for the results. Daddy had been practicing his *"black, sock, adore"* test. He had even written it down and practiced so he could pass the test. It was his cheat sheet for the exam. The doctor never asked him about it, so Daddy volunteered, "I remember, black, sock," looking at my mom, saying, "what is the last word?" She said, "adore" and he said, "I know that. It's adore." He was proud of himself for remembering. The doctor said, "That's good Mr. Carlin. You don't have to remember it anymore." Daddy was miffed. He wanted to prove he was okay. We were about to find out he was far from okay.

The doctor said all the test results indicated Daddy had Alzheimer's disease and possibly Lewy body dementia, a terrible disease with symptoms of both Alzheimer's and Parkinson's.

I was shocked. In my mind all I could think was, *"What did he just say? That can't be right. He said Parkinson's. He won't forget me with Parkinson's."*

The doctor opened a binder with a series of MRI images on one page and a larger MRI image on the opposite page.

"This is a picture of your brain from your MRI, Mr. Carlin. If you compare it to this series of MRIs showing the progression of Alzheimer's, you can see you are about here."

He ran his finger across the top row down to the middle of the second row out of three. Daddy looked confused.

I was confused.

We all sat silently.

"So, did you get the pictures of my head back?"

"Mr. Carlin. This is a picture of your brain."

The picture he pointed to so matter-of-factly was quite confusing. It looked like a cross-section of cauliflower, not like the somewhat smooth brain in the first box of the group of images on the opposite page. The brain in the first box filled the skull and looked healthy. The brain belonging to my dad didn't look like it at all. It was jagged around the edges, and there were two dark circles near the bottom section and a large, dark "T" in the middle.

"So, are you going to show me my pictures?"

The doctor again said that the pictures he was looking at were his. Daddy asked three or four more times, and the doctor patiently answered him the same each time. I was with Daddy on this one. It didn't seem real. It looked like something you see after an autopsy. I was hoping the answer would be different every time Daddy asked. He was hopeful, too.

The doctor explained that the dark circles were the areas in his brain where his memory was located. He showed us the dark, jagged area at the front of his skull. He said that as Daddy's brain cells deteriorated, his cognitive-reasoning area in the front of his brain took over to help him remember things through a series of steps. Because he was highly educated and had a cerebral-type job, the cognitive-reasoning portion of his brain had been very strong. That was why we hadn't noticed any drastic changes in him until now. He said that when his frontal lobe became atrophied, he lost the ability to cover for the memory loss and to fully utilize his cognitive functions. This explained why his decline seemed to happen so quickly, when in fact, it had been going on for years. We had an explanation, but not one I wanted. It was a diagnosis of a fatal, non-curable disease. I don't know how much Daddy comprehended. He seemed so confused. What does anyone really understand when they are given a death sentence? Poor guy. I can't imagine what was going through his mind, his now disabled and diseased mind. I know he had to be fearful, but he never said anything. He was silent.

We were all stunned.

This was mid-July, 2013. I was scheduled to speak to the ladies at our church on the following Sunday evening. I had brought my laptop with me on the trip to work on the slideshow presentation to accompany my talk. I was teaching about the word "Hallelujah." On praise. How could I praise when I couldn't breathe? My dad was going to suffer and die. He was going to forget me and stop loving me. I was not thankful at all and not singing hallelujah about anything. And now I had to get up in front of all these precious women and pretend I'm praising God and tell them to praise God, also.

I wasn't mad at God. I didn't blame Him. I just felt too broken to say nice things or be joyful. Until that time, I saw praise as happy, joyful things we say to God. I was none of those things. I was numb. I was in mourning. I had just been thrown into the Pain stage of grief. As I prayed and prepared to teach, I was also praying to understand what was happening. I realized God was with our family. I had to learn to praise even in the dark time of my life. I had to honor Him for who He was, not how I felt.

Research showed me that Daddy had already moved into stage 4 of his battle. He had clear signs and symptoms of Alzheimer's disease. His thinking and reasoning issues had become more visible, and he had new difficulties every day. The global deterioration scale calls this the Moderate stage.[8]

Chapter 13

The Battle Begins

As Daddy always did when he needed to conquer something, he started researching and making notes. He built his arsenal. He got on the computer and began looking for information on alternative causes for the issues we told him he was experiencing. He wasn't convinced he had symptoms of any kind, but he looked, none the less. He pulled articles about treatments for all his possible ailments. And he researched Alzheimer's disease. A friend, the one whom he had forgotten three years prior at his retirement party, owned long-term care facilities and was very well acquainted with the disease. He gave Dad the book, <u>Mayo Clinic on Alzheimer's Disease</u>[9]. Dad read through this book many times. By looking through the book, now covered in highlighter, underlines, notes and dog-eared pages, you can see into his thoughts and heart.

The first reading is evident through the sharp, somewhat straight highlights of neon orange. Occasionally there is a note written legibly and an arrow pointing to a fact he wanted to remember.

Another reading is marked using a red pen and more notes. There are two pictures under the heading *"How Alzheimer's disease progresses."* One picture is of a healthy brain. The other is the brain of a person in the moderate stage of the disease. Daddy wrote "*Important*" in red and drew arrows to both. He had no idea how important it would be. The diseased brain in the second picture had a distinct heart-shaped cavity in the middle, just like the image of his brain that I chose for the cover of this book to represent his strong heart. The red underlining in this reading was much more wide-spread than the orange highlight. It sometimes reinforced his attention to an already highlighted sentence or fact. The red pen was used to mark quotations around "no cure" and to underline those dreadful words with two short lines. Also, double underlined was the phrase, "*Alzheimer's is persistent and becomes more severe over time.*" An arrow pointed to it as well. "*Visit your doctor*" got three lines. The phrase "*help keep you alive*" got an arrow and the word, "*yes.*" Unfortunately, it was talking about metabolism, not a cure. The words "*Unrelenting*" and "*Irreversible*" had a neon orange highlight, red lines, and red circles. They caused him grief and strong feelings as he took out his frustration with his pens.

As his disease progressed, he continued to re-read the book. It's interesting to me that I could see his decline by noticing how his once, somewhat straight lines, became haphazard and messy, almost scribbled. He switched to a faded pink highlighter, a red pencil, and a blue pen. I wonder if he continued reading to find the paragraph of hope that he may have missed the times before, or if he was trying to find himself in the stages and descriptions of a slow decline to the point in which he would no longer be able to think and reason.

He never talked to my sister nor me about what he read. I asked my Mom if they had talked about his feelings about the disease. She said, "No. He denied he had Alzheimer's, so we didn't talk about it." I think I would like to know what was going through his mind, but then I don't know if I would have been able to handle hearing the agony he was experiencing.

The only thing he ever repeated from the book was the mention of life expectancy. The sentence reads, *"As noted earlier in the chapter, death occurs, on average, about 8 to 10 years following the initial diagnosis of Alzheimer's by a doctor."*[10] It was marked with orange highlighter, red lines, blue lines and an arrow to a note *"See page 35 about diagnosis."* He was doing the math to see how long, or short, the remainder of his life would be. He would repeat this sentence frequently, always through gritted teeth and with a scowl on his face. His obsession with living to be 93 became more prevalent, and he became more determined.

He turned to God for healing and understanding. He knew where his comfort came from and it was from the Lord. For many years, before going to church on Sundays, he watched Rev. Charles Stanley from the First Baptist Church in Atlanta, Georgia preach on television. He also read his monthly publications and listened to his cassettes, then CDs. I would laugh and say Daddy thought of Charles Stanley as the Baptist pope. He underlined, circled, drew arrows, and wrote notes on all of Charles Stanley's In Touch Ministries information. He trusted God more than he believed the doctors.

―――――

When we went back for the first visit after the initial diagnosis, he was armed for the fight. He had the tan, expandable portfolio he carried when he worked for clients, full of medical and biblical information. The doctor started asking how things were and asking us about any changes. We had to be honest with him. We had to tell him about things Daddy was doing that were out of the ordinary. He didn't smile at us like he did the first time we openly betrayed him.

I couldn't make eye contact. Julie would hold his hand and pat him. It didn't make him less hurt or mad.

When it was his time to talk, he showed the doctor the information he had prepared. Daddy was schooling him on all things Alzheimer's. The doctor thanked him but didn't act interested in what he had brought or what he had to say. It was a little rude, but he didn't have the same need or responsibility to make Daddy feel validated and dignified that I did. Then Daddy pulled out his information from Charles Stanley. He tells the doctor, "I'm a Christian, and I believe that God is going to heal me. I'm praying, and I'm reading scriptures. Charles Stanley said God can heal us and I believe him because it's in the bible."

The doctor, again, was uninterested.

"Faith is a good thing, Mr. Carlin, but we need to talk about treatment and what is going on with you."

Daddy looked at me and said, "This guy doesn't even believe in God!"

He was sad.

He was mad. No, he was furious.

He was not going to be hopeless even though the situation was hopeless. He was going to fight. He had been fighting his entire life. As a middle child of five boys, as a boxer, for my mother's love, to gain the respect of his father, to be heard and appreciated at work, to buy the land he loved, and to raise my sister and me to become successful and happy adults. He was going to fight this diagnosis. He would not waver from his will to live and to find something to stop the progression of the disease. He refused to acknowledge its existence.

The doctor read him the report from the psychologist. It said he had mild to moderate impairment. That made him really angry. He couldn't believe that woman would say those things about him. He thought she liked him. He didn't understand that she was basing her opinion on the tests and that she did like him. She was mean to him, in his mind. He was so hurt. He was mad at Julie and me for making him go to the doctor in the first place because nothing was wrong with him.

He never owned Alzheimer's disease. He ignored it and talked about it like something other people had, but not him. The people around him were wrong. The doctor was wrong. He told you so, pointing his finger at you and talking through gritted teeth.

He continued driving for a short time after his diagnosis. Since he thought he was fine, he would hop in his truck and take off. It was scary, but he was determined he could drive, and we couldn't stop him. He and mom fought about it every day. We'd make excuses for us to take him places or for mom to drive. We had to do something because he apparently was having problems and having wrecks. But he was headstrong and obstinate. He was not going to listen to the doctor because "*he didn't know what he was talking about.*"

Mom, Julie, and I talked to the doctor's nurse behind Daddy's back and told her the doctor needed to take away his driver license. We were afraid he would hurt someone or hurt himself. During that appointment, the doctor finally told him, "Mr. Carlin. You can no longer drive a vehicle. Your disease makes it difficult for you to comprehend things and your reaction time is slow." Daddy clenched his teeth and glared at him. His freedom was being taken away from him shortly after the devastating diagnosis. He was angry, confused, and in denial of his condition.

"*The doctor is stupid. There is nothing wrong with me. I can drive if I want.*"

Mom didn't want to take away his keys because "he knows enough to know if I take them off of his ring." She knew it would be a fight. So, the truck just sat in the driveway while we all worried if he was going to drive off and get hurt. He threatened to take it around the block all the time. He'd say, "I'm just going to back it out of the driveway, circle around the block and I'll pull right back in." His free-will had just been revoked. He couldn't run to breakfast at his current daily stop, Whataburger. He couldn't run to his woods on Saturday. He had to depend on mother or one of us to take him. He had been so independent; now, he was dependent. The daily battle had become so stressful on Mom. Once she heard the truck start and ran outside just in time to see him pulling out of the driveway. He drove around the block and came back home, proving he was fit to drive. Mother disagreed. So did her neighbor, who is a police officer. He told Dad that if he saw him driving, he would have to arrest him. He would never do that, but they were trying to keep him from getting behind the wheel.

As far as we know, he never actually drove the truck again. He told us constantly that he was going to, but I don't think he ever did. Even with all the anger and defiance, he followed the rules. No matter how stupid he thought the new rule was, he followed it because that's how he was. His integrity governed his final decisions. He had been told "No," so he didn't.

In September of 2013, he went to renew his driver license because it was expiring on his birthday. He declared he was going to get another license and drive his truck.

The DMV worker asked, "Have you ever been told by a doctor that you are not to drive?"

"Yes. The doctor said I have Alzheimer's, but I don't, so I can still drive."

The lady told him she could not give him a driver license, but she would give him an identification card instead. Again, he was angry. That's a recurring theme during this time, if you haven't noticed. When your freedom and dignity and lifestyle are robbed from you, anger is a natural reaction. He had his driver license number memorized, and he'd rattle it off to you to prove he was okay. He tried to remember the ID card number, but I don't think he ever did.

He continued to insist he could and would drive. He was determined to go back to the doctor, have him give him more tests, and he would pass all the tests and get his driver's license back, proving we were all wrong. He repeated this over and over, resulting in many clashes with Mom.

I know the battle of taking away someone's driver license is something the loved ones of Alzheimer's victims all have and it's one of the first times they must make a hard decision to take over care for that person. As Mom said, the person with Alzheimer's at this point generally knows enough to not be easily "tricked" into not driving. They want to continue with life as usual, although they are unable to make sound decisions. They do not see the decline in themselves that is so evident to others. I have a friend who couldn't stop his Dad from driving. He continued to get behind the wheel and would end up in a ditch. The police would get involved, and it would be an ugly scene. Another friend's dad drives from his house to breakfast every morning. So far, he's done okay, but what about the day he possibly gets lost or hurt or hurts someone else. How do you tell your parent, "*No!*" Unless you have had to face this situation, you cannot answer that question. It's not, "*Just Say No.*" There are too many moving parts and emotions. Too many brain cells left, but not enough to park safely between the lines.

Now, what to do about the truck? Since he couldn't drive and didn't have a license, it was a waste of money paying a note and insurance on a vehicle he didn't use. Doug and I went to their house, and the three of us took pictures of his shiny, clean truck. We posted it for sale online, and it sold immediately. He was so sad to see it go but loved that the man who bought it told him how pretty it was and how excited he was to buy it from him. Daddy talked about buying a new truck. The dark blue truck he sold became a yellow one in his mind, but he wanted to repurchase his independence. He argued with Mom and told her the doctor didn't say he couldn't drive. At a subsequent visit, Mom told the doctor about the daily arguments and Daddy's denial that the doctor told him he couldn't drive. The doctor wrote Dad a note on a prescription pad, *"Mr. Carlin is no longer allowed to drive."* When he gave us a hard time about driving, we'd show him the note. He'd say, *"That's a crock,"* one of his non-cursing curse-word phrases. He continued to cut out truck sale ads from the paper, and he continued to ask the doctor to give him back his driver's license. That strive for freedom continued until a few weeks before he died.

Chapter 14

Obsessions And Fixations

Pre-Alzheimer's, Dad was sharp. He was quick-witted and good with numbers. He loved accounting and never met a stranger or forgot a friend. As his disease progressed, this accountant who had been responsible for millions of dollars forgot how to handle money issues properly. He started ordering all kinds of things online, from magazines, and as advertised on television.

He ordered magazines and renewed the ones he had at the prompting of a popular sweepstakes company. I know they didn't guarantee he would win, but he thought that it became a sure-thing if he ordered the magazines. Mom walked into the office one day as he was yelling at some poor call-center worker. He had received a, *"You may have won $40,000"* letter in the mail. He wanted his money. He needed it, and they were obligated to send him a check, now! Mom asked to speak to the person. He fought her but eventually gave her the phone. She told the person on the other end of the line that Daddy had Alzheimer's and to please take him off their mailing list. He was furious and embarrassed. He yelled at her for telling them that he had Alzheimer's, which he didn't, and for not insisting they give him the money they owed him. Mom and Dad were getting *Rolling Stone* and *Seventeen* magazines along with all other kinds of publications they wouldn't usually order. Mom was getting renewal slips in the mail, so I began calling the subscription company and asking them to remove him from their list and to stop his subscription. I found out they were third-party companies and they had no control over his orders or subscriptions. They would sell a renewal, and it would be added on top of the existing subscription. He had some deer-hunting magazines with paid-up subscriptions for 17 years. When talking to him on the phone, it was evident that he had issues. But there are unscrupulous and evil people in the world who have no problem preying on people like him. The major sweepstakes company didn't mind his continued business, either. He ordered all kinds of stuff from them. I was in his office once and asked why he had a light that attached to his ball cap sitting on his desk. He told me he had to buy it so they could send him the money they owed him. It made me sick that he was so blatantly ripped off. I finally got him off all these lists, but they will continue to receive the magazines for the entirety of the subscription.

He also would tell people his Social Security number and driver license number. He couldn't really hear what they were saying, and he just volunteered everything he knew. He still remembered them and wanted everyone to see he was still capable and smart. Mom heard him giving his Social Security number to someone over the phone. She ran in the office and found he had called to order something he found online or in the mail. He was giving them all the numbers he could remember and the ones he read off the cheat sheets on his desk.

Mom eventually let his credit card expire and didn't renew it in an attempt to stop his shopping. After his credit card had been revoked, Mom heard him trying to order something else over the phone. He told the operator on the other line, "Just send it to me, and I'll send you a check." He argued with the person on the other line, "Yes, you can do that. Why not?" He also donated money to any and everyone who sent him a *"please give"* card or called. He would buy whatever you had to sell if you had a story to go along with your pitch. He still had a benevolent heart.

It was his money, and he could do with it as he pleased. Or, so he said. He was trying to live life the way he always had, but things just weren't the same.

Daddy began fixating on things and repeating them over and over. He was obsessed with his cousin, Murlene, with whom he had grown up with and had recently reconnected. He wanted to read their email exchange from several years ago so he could write to her. He'd ask me to come over and find it because he couldn't. I looked and couldn't locate it, either. That didn't stop him from calling every day for several weeks to ask me to come over and dig through his old emails. Because he clicked everything on the internet, he often ended up with viruses, even with virus protection software. The emails from Murlene probably got lost during one of the virus-scrubs either the computer store or I did on their system.

He liked to go back and look at old tests and grade sheets from when he taught accounting. He'd pull the files and mess with them. Sometimes he'd end up deleting things and saving the changes. When he couldn't find it again, he'd call me. When the computer got to be too much for him, he'd pull out papers he had saved for years from his file cabinets. He'd re-read the budget presentation he did for the energy company from back in the mid-1970s. He'd take out and review old tax returns he prepared. He even had a canceled check from when I started college in 1984. He had it sitting on top of his pile of papers and would show it to me when I was there visiting. Later, he put it under the glass to keep it safe. He liked reminiscing. He enjoyed reliving and remembering things from the past. Moments and accomplishments he was proud of, like the budget and his time teaching. Anytime he found something and pulled it out of a drawer or cabinet, it ended up on his desk. Therefore, it was covered with random papers that spanned 40 years of memories.

His weight was another obsession. He wasn't fat. But he hadn't missed any pancakes, burgers, or ice cream in a long time. He would weigh himself once in the morning and once in the evening, recording the readings in a small calendar book. He'd announce when he gained point four pounds or lost one point eight pounds. He started pointing out people's bellies, to their faces. Weight was just something he liked to talk about. And hair. He was proud that he had a full head of hair. He would point out how much hair he had while telling someone they were bald. No one with thinning hair was spared. He wasn't mean. It was the opposite. He was making conversation. He had forgotten what appropriate conversation was and what might get him punched in the nose.

As mentioned before, Daddy was obsessed with living to be 93 years old, just like his Dad. He talked about him quite a bit. My PaPaw was a tough man. He and his sister were raised by a single mom, and at a very young age, he had to work to support himself. He told me a story about his mom packing his bag and taking him to the main road in Port Arthur, Texas where they lived. From there she helped him hitchhike a ride to the train station in Beaumont, Texas, about 30 miles away. He got on a train and road it to New Iberia, Louisiana, where his father lived in a boarding house. When he got there, his Dad was gone off to work. The lady that owned the house let him stay in his dad's room and cared for him until his Dad returned. Not too bad of a story until you find out he was only five years old.

Jimmy "The Kid" Carlin was a fighter. A boxer in the ring and scraper on the street. He went by J.W. and was a handsome, dark-haired man. His rough childhood and subsequent life choices made him a rigid, abrasive individual. My dad was the middle child of J.W.'s kids. Pat was born during his first marriage and Wayne, Ronnie, Philip, and David from his second. The first two and last two boys looked just like him. Coal-black hair, light olive skin, and handsome. Daddy had white blond hair, fair skin, and crystal blue eyes like his mom. PaPaw would make MaMaw carry my Daddy when they were in public, so people wouldn't wonder why he looked so different from the other boys.

Daddy liked boxing, just like his father, and bragged on his Golden Gloves wins. He was a kid, a skinny kid, during his prize-winning career with his dad as the coach of the team. My PaPaw was rude and critical. He would tell you to "*shut up*" in the middle of a conversation and in front of other people. He was also sweet sometimes. I was the only one of the ten grandkids who spent any extended time with him. He'd tell me I was fat and I'd say he was old. He'd laugh. He liked the banter. It was like loving an old, cranky mutt that would love on you for a while and then turn and nip you because you moved a certain way. If you have an old, jerk dog, you may be able to understand my reason for hanging out with him. He'd tell me stories about his growing up and about my Dad's mom who had died at only 55 years of age. I reminded him of her, he said. We favor a little bit, especially when I see myself in a mirror with no expression on my face. She was a sad, depressed woman, and she suffered from mental illness for many years. Depression overtook her completely when her son, Philip, was killed in a car wreck at the young age of 22. Her goal in life, after Philip died, was to die on the same day as he died. She finally got her wish. She died on September 16. He had died on September 15. Both were a couple of days before my Dad's birthday.

I'm grateful to have had a relationship with my grandfather. Sometimes it's easier to love someone who tries so hard to be unlovable when you know the background behind their destructive behavior. I sometimes wonder what in his past caused him to be so terrible to everyone. It was his first instinct when interacting with someone. He attacked with no mercy. But in contrast, he told me that he got on his knees every day and prayed for each of his grandkids. When his knees gave out, he sat in a chair to pray. *"God can hear me from the chair, too,"* he told me. In his oxymoronic way, he would pray for you in the morning and then would say what you were doing wrong or thinking wrong or anything ugly that came to his mind. He would say it to your face; like spitting in your face with words. He had a very dysfunctional relationship with everyone.

I never saw him be kind to my Dad. They'd talk hunting and fishing and golf. But then, he'd belittle my Dad's accomplishments, tell him he was stupid, and say he couldn't do anything right. He'd take every opportunity to tear him down. Unprovoked and intentional. He was so nasty to his sons. However, it was my Dad who stopped by his house every morning to move the newspaper from the driveway to the back door, so MaMaw could just open the door and pick it up. It was my Dad who visited him every week and would mow his grass. It was my Dad who lived in town and was there any time he was needed. It was my Dad whom he verbally abused on a constant basis. It was my Dad who took his daily tirades but continued to respect him as his Dad.

HE WAS

Right before PaPaw's 93rd birthday, in November, 2009, he had to move into a nursing home. His knees were making it impossible for him to stand and walk and his wife, Kathryn, whom he married after my dad's mother died, was having health issues that made it impossible for her to care for him. He had been in the nursing home about a week when he celebrated his birthday. Several family members gathered at the facility in a dining room, brought in food and cake and had a party. Daddy was wheeling him down the hallway headed to see his guests. PaPaw was fussing at him for not pushing the wheelchair right and for being a loser. He never let up with the hatefulness.

PaPaw once asked me why I thought God was making him live so long with macular degeneration and acute hearing loss. He said it was like living in the Twilight Zone, seeing and hearing things he couldn't really see and hear.

"God is giving you one last opportunity to stop being mean and to say something nice."

He laughed and said, "I suppose so."

Twenty-two days later, PaPaw died in his sleep. The night before, my husband had stopped by to see him. He called me and told PaPaw, "Guess who's on the phone? It's Denise."

"Tell Denise I love her."

"I love you too, PaPaw."

I guess he finally said something nice.

Daddy struggled with PaPaw's death. I think it was because he never found reconciliation with him. When we were filling out the online questionnaire for his first psychologist visit, I asked him the question, *"Have you ever sought help from a therapist?"* He said yes. I was a little shocked and asked, when? He told me a general date and said, "I was trying to figure out why I couldn't get along with my Dad." I told him, "It's because he was a jerk. It wasn't your fault." He looked at me with sad eyes and didn't say anything else. He wanted his father's love and approval. He never received it.

When Daddy read the ten-year life-expectancy, he said, "I am going to live to be 93, just like my dad." He repeated this over and over throughout the years. At his birthday I said, "You are 72 today." He'd say, "Good. And I'm going to live to be 93, just like my dad."

PaPaw's mind was sharp as a razor when he died, just like his tongue. I'm not sure which was worse, being lucid and clear in your mind as your body fails and slowly dies, or your mind failing so you don't know you are slowly dying.

And I'm aware that I've talked about him wanting to live to be 93 several times. It was the most repeated obsession we heard from him. We heard it over and over and over. Even more than wanting a new truck. He wanted to live.

Another obsession was little kids. He loved little kids and wanted them to give him a high-five. He'd talk to every kid he saw, much to the dismay of my Mom. She would tell him, "People don't want strangers talking to their kids. It scares them." He didn't listen to her. Sometimes he wouldn't stop talking, even after the parent was trying to get away. He would get his feelings hurt when they wouldn't respond or if he didn't get to talk as long as he wanted. Once when we were going to his doctor, we arrived in town early to have lunch with my daughter, Lauren. We met her in the parking garage of her office and ate at the restaurant around the corner. Daddy was already fidgety and anxious because he was nervous. He hated going to the doctor. He saw a little boy at one of the tables across the restaurant. He got up from the table and made a beeline to this kid. We couldn't stop him. He was friendly and sweet, but the parents were obviously uncomfortable. We found out, the hard way, that if you intercepted him or tried to make him stop, he would get loud and belligerent. It was best to approach him gently and try to bring the conversation to a close by saying goodbye to the people he approached and moving away slowly, redirecting his attention to something near where he was supposed to be. It was so difficult and embarrassing. I wasn't ashamed or embarrassed by him. I didn't want people to think poorly of him. He couldn't help it, and he was just being nice.

The kids who sat in front of my parents at church called him "The Candy Man." He always had peppermints or other hard candy he took from a restaurant, mixed with the napkins he also collected from the restaurant, in his pocket. He would give it to them to keep them quiet and to be nice. Doug and I moved our membership to my parent's church in 2010. The First Baptist Church of Groves, Texas had been an integral part of my family for many years. My parents met there in Sunday School. They were baptized there. They were married there. My sister and I started our membership there as babies in the nursery. Grew up there. I'm one of the pianists there. I was the financial secretary there for a few years. FBC Groves is our family.

Every Sunday morning, after praise & worship, I would take my seat on the pew with Doug and my parents. Daddy would reach over and hand me a mint. Every. Single. Sunday. Even after he began to decline, he passed out mints. If he could catch my eye while I was playing, he'd pull the mint out of his pocket and show it to me with a big, excited smile. Such a sweetie. One Sunday, when he was deep into the

Alzheimer's fog, he stood up while the pastor was giving announcements and started walking up to the stage where I was sitting at the piano. My mother was trying to stop him, but he started flailing his arms to get away from her. Loudly he said, "Shut up! Leave me alone. Stop telling me what to do!" When he got away from her, he turned toward me with a beautiful smile, holding up the candy and walked up to me. He was so excited to give it to me. I smiled and said, "Thank you, Daddy. I love you. I'll come to sit with you in a second." He said, "Okay, Shug" and headed back to the pew. His disease was not a secret among our FBC family. At least it wasn't anymore.

His obsessions grew worse as the disease progressed. The filter that gave him a mental stopping point seemed to dissipate into thin air. By the time the most intense obsessions and actions took place, he had moved into Stage Five. His fixations were manifested out of his desire to be kind and friendly and to love people. His heart was so loving, and his smile was so big. His mind didn't know how to handle all the love his heart was trying to give. In looking at how he freely loved everyone during this time, it makes me think that having a filter isn't always the best.

Chapter 15

Speaking With No Filter

Right before he ended his teaching career, he would call out the young men with their pants hanging down. He would tell them to wear a belt to his class. Because he had always been a sharp dresser, I genuinely think he thought they just didn't have belts. He even told the man at the counter at Whataburger to pull up his pants and to wear a belt. The young man said he didn't own a belt. My dad brought him one the next day. He's lucky no one ever pushed back too hard about his fashion advice. He was very free and diligent to give it to all the young men he met. He hated when I wore flip-flops. They were not the rubber kind, but he would tell me, "Those shoes are ugly. Don't wear them anymore." Then he'd point out that I had little feet like my mom.

In the fifth and sixth stages of his disease, his internal social filter went away. He began pointing out things about people that were glaring, but you didn't talk about. To the lady asking him medical questions, he said, "Hey. You have a big mole right there on the side of your chin. Right there." Sometimes he'd point or make a sad face or a yuck face, but most of the time it was just a statement. Just making observations and conversation.

We met a nice older man at Whataburger while having lunch together on a Saturday. He was friendly and was offering us ketchup and extra napkins. He was also missing a few teeth on the top, in the front of his mouth. My daddy said, "You don't have no teeth over there." He made the yuck face. It was so awkward. The man just smiled while I made the *"he has Alzheimer's and doesn't mean to be rude"* face. Daddy then said, "I don't have teeth in the back" as he pulled out his partial to show him. His declaration of the man's imperfection wasn't an insult. It was the beginning of a relatable condition. *"I'm missing teeth, too!"* It got kind of funny as Daddy kept wanting him to look at his fake back teeth. He said it several times, so it remained awkward. Uncomfortable situations just happened. You roll with them, hope the unsuspecting third party isn't offended, and you move on. Luckily, I never witnessed anyone being rude to him.

He liked teeth. Starting at the beginning of his journey, he straight-up, unashamedly flirted with waitresses and pretty girls in general. He would tell them, "You sure have pretty blue eyes. I have blue eyes, too." He added to the conversation a little later, "You sure have pretty teeth. Did you have braces?" As he moved further down the road of decline, he would say, "You sure have pretty teeth. Did your Daddy buy you those?" He was obsessed with pretty teeth and fathers paying for braces. It's funny because neither Julie nor I had braces. He would tell me, *"You have pretty teeth. Did I buy those for you?"* I'd say, "Nope. God did." He'd get a big laugh out of it. The further he regressed, the broader his compliment base grew. He started commenting on guys' teeth, too. He never told them they had pretty eyes, but he noticed everyone's teeth. I don't remember when he stopped commenting on teeth and eyes. But as much as I hated it in the beginning, it's sad to know it stopped.

My dad always kissed us. It was a peck kiss, and it's a Cajun thing that everyone does and has for generations. It's our hello and goodbye. Daddy had become obsessed with kissing. He wasn't inappropriate with the kiss. It wasn't sexual or anything. It was him being excited to see you. However, he started hello-kissing women outside the family. I think since he was having trouble remembering who was family and who was not, he just kissed everyone. The couple of ladies he smooched knew him and knew what he was struggling with mentally. They loved him and did not feel offended. But you could see the sadness in their eyes for us. We finally had to tell him that he could only kiss his wife. He could no longer kiss us or anyone else. Just Mom. He would forget, but we held firm. It was hard because we denied him an expression of love toward us. We denied ourselves as well. He always looked sad when we said, "*No kissing*." We had to break his habit.

I had been working at my job for a few months when we had a resource fair that was open to the public. My mom wanted to see where I worked, so she and my dad came to the event. When they picked me up for lunch before the fair, my dad wanted to give me a kiss.

"No kiss today. I've been sick, and I have a cold."

"So, no kiss? How about I kiss you on the neck?"

I laughed. "No kissing on the neck, either."

He didn't understand. "Why not?"

"No kissing. No kissing on the neck. Just give me a hug. You can only kiss Mom."

He gave me a hug but seemed sad, as if I were being mean to him. Like he was trying to figure out what he did wrong and why he got in trouble.

After lunch, we came back to the resource fair. I introduced my parents to people from the community and my new co-workers. My dad proceeded to tell several people, "This is my daughter. I raised her. I kiss her on the neck sometimes, but not today because she's sick." He would then offer to kiss them on the neck. Not cool at all! I would whisper behind his back the obvious explanation, *"He has Alzheimer's."* People were understanding and sweet. I work at a behavioral health facility. My co-workers have seen everything and are kind and caring people. He loved walking around meeting new people and telling them he raised me. He was all about the free cookies and candy, too. He was so proud of me, and that was how he verbalized it. I loved his bragging on me.

Before his diagnosis, he was always friendly to waitstaff, learning their names, and laughing and talking to them. He and my Mom would make friends with the waiters everywhere they ate. It was sweet and strange at the same time. They knew the people's name and their business, and their families. They even went to the wedding of one of their favorite waiters and hostess wife. Everyone loved them, and they tipped well, so I guess it was okay.

Daddy's fun and friendly interaction with the young waiters and waitresses started to change not long before we had a diagnosis to explain it. If a young server said, *"no problem"* in response to his *"thank you,"* he would say, "Well, I have a problem with you saying you have no problem. You are supposed to say you are welcome. Not no problem." The poor kid would say, *"You're welcome"* and quickly sneak away from the table. Every single time he made a big deal out of it. And the deal got bigger and bigger as time progressed. For him to harass a waiter about "*no problem*" was out of character. Social butterflies like my parents were always friendly, not confrontational.

Another thing he did was order limes for his water. He had done that for a while. But then he started asking the servers, "Do you know why I get limes?" The answer is because limes don't usually have seeds. No seeds to clog up your straw like when you squeeze lemons in your water. One poor, young waiter took our order at a local, nice restaurant. Daddy ordered a bowl of limes for his water. Then he asked the kid, "Do you know why I get limes instead of lemons?"

"No, sir."

"Limes don't have seeds like lemons do. I'll pay you five dollars if you can find a lime with a seed in it."

The waiter took the challenge. It wasn't his best idea. You see, Daddy looked normal, talked normal, and was just seemingly being friendly. The poor kid had no idea what was lurking beneath the surface. He proudly returned to the table after a few minutes with a lime on a small plate, with a seed in it.

"I found a lime with a seed! You owe me five dollars."

Oh my goodness. My Daddy went from zero to ballistic in two point three seconds.

"I don't owe you anything! Get away from me and take your lime."

The kid thought he was joking and pressed on. "But you said if I find a lime with a seed in it, you would pay me five dollars. I looked through every lime in the bar and found one."

Daddy was red and mad. We were all looking at the waiter, shaking our heads, mouthing, "*We're sorry! Please go. Walk away. STOP TALKING.*" The young man looked so defeated. He thought he had won a game. Daddy thought someone humiliated and disrespected him, or so he felt, by proving he was wrong. He was so sensitive in his awareness that he was slipping and no longer fully functioning. It was early after his diagnosis. He didn't discuss his thoughts, but we saw them ignite in the restaurant. He wouldn't speak to the waiter anymore that evening and refused to tip him. The kid ended up getting a big tip from the rest of us at the table.

His social awkwardness became more pronounced as his disease progressed. Eventually, he and Mom stopped going out to eat. Family gatherings took place at home, rather than restaurants. Mom tried to keep doing things as they always had. This included going out for dinner on the weekends. It was hard on her when they had to stop.

They had to stop going to the weekly church service, too. They went to Sunday School because it was a place where Mom could be social, and Daddy was in a group of men who loved him and protected him during their hour together. He started being loud in the service, arguing with Mom and talking to Doug or me. The last time they came, he leaned up and was playing with a girl's hair in front of him. She wasn't even a member of the church. She was a visitor with some other people who came to see their relative be baptized.

With this disease, so many things happen that are uncomfortable and awkward. Like I said earlier, I wasn't ashamed of him. Ever. I didn't want people to judge him or disrespect him or think less of him. He couldn't help himself.

Chapter 16

His Fears And Mine

When I was working on this book, I attended a writing conference in Sedona, Arizona. Everything was going great the first day until after lunch. I was able to finish up where I had left off before we left for our meal. But, when I tried to move on to the next subject, I was blank. More than blank. I just sat there, struggling to write something. I wrote a few facts, but I couldn't bring my words together. My mind felt frozen. I could see an image of my Dad's face, but I couldn't see details or put words to what I saw. I knew the memory was there, but I couldn't reach it or touch it or put emotion to it. I felt choked and suffocated.

"What is happening? What is wrong with me? I have to get out of here."

I needed to stand up and get out of the room. Not in an anxious way but because I was suffocating. I needed to breathe and clear my head, so I walked out into the lobby and hesitated. I wanted someone to ask if I was okay so I could say "no," get a hug, and cry a little bit. I needed something.

I walked around outside but didn't find a place to land. I walked back inside, waited for someone to hug me and then walked into the great room, standing against the wall in the back. I watched all the workshop attendees typing and engaged in their writing. I could feel the creativity and energy in the room. It was something I could physically sense. The daughter of our host and teacher popped by a few times. She seemed so free and light. She was telling her dad about the tea she made from a plant in the garden. I like free and light. But I felt weighted and oppressed at that moment. My mind was heavy, slow, and confused. Tom, our host, stopped by and said, "Walk outside and get some fresh air." I told him, "I did, but it's hot." He laughed. Eventually, I walked through the lobby, headed outside. Tom did some jumping jacks, as if to wake me up. I shook my head "no" and said, "I'm struggling," as I walked past him. I went outside again and up on the rooftop walk path. I found a chair at the end of the path. It was a shaded spot that looked over one of the mountains. It had a magnificent view of the mountains surrounding the city. I always sing, *"These Thousand Hills"* by Third Day when I see mountains. They are the footprints of God.

As I looked at the mountain and asked God why I was having such a terrible time, I closed my eyes. I thought of the struggle going on in my head. I then heard in my spirit, *"You are feeling his struggle. You are feeling his heart."* Daddy struggled with putting his thoughts together on a much bigger scale and for many years. He tried to remember things he knew he was supposed to know. But the memory wouldn't show itself. He was suffocated and crushed by the inability to move forward.

I saw his heart. His strong heart. I felt his heart. I felt a small amount of his struggle. I couldn't think fully, but I loved fully, enough to want to complete this book for him and for others needing a kindred spirit. It was paralyzing and painful.

I cried from deep in my stomach. I asked the Lord, *"Did he cry? Did he ask you why?"* I know he asked to be healed. *"What was he feeling?"* Poor soul. How torturous this had been for him.

A small glimpse or feeling of being lost and incomplete is frightening. I'm frightened by the possibility of developing Alzheimer's. According to scientists, beta-amyloid plaques can start developing twenty years before symptoms are manifested[11]. The plaques break down the ability of the neurons in the brain to fire and function properly. If Daddy was starting to exhibit symptoms at age sixty-six, he could have possibly been forty-six when it all began. I'm fifty-two. I sometimes struggle with finding the right word to say when speaking. I fight to remember names and numbers even though I was sharp at one time. I memorized music quickly and easily when I was young. I tried to memorize a song a few weeks ago, and I kept playing the four-measure introduction over and over. I never quite got it. I know I'm older. I know I think a lot for work and in life in general. I always have traffic in my mind. Lately, there have been some jams and fender benders. It scares me. I know my family loves me, but I do not want my family to have to care for me. I don't want to be the person wandering around the restaurant like Daddy was, talking to people and making them uncomfortable. I don't want to forget Lauren or Doug or anybody else. I don't want to be helpless and sad, just a shell of my former self. When I say all those things that I don't want my family to go through, I realize, I have gone through them all.

Did I resent Daddy for putting us through this? Absolutely not. I hurt for him. I would do anything for him. I tried to protect him. I don't say I don't want my family to have to go through Alzheimer's again with me because I was sorry I had to go through it with Daddy. I was sorry for him. It's for selfish reasons I'm afraid of Alzheimer's. I don't want to die like that. Alzheimer's takes away a person's dignity, respect, pride, freedom, sense of self. I don't want to not be me.

Alzheimer's kills who the person was because it destroys the brain. Everything that makes us who we are is stored in the brain and in memories. Alzheimer's is like a flood that destroys everything that was inside of a house as the waters rise. The frame is still there when the floodwaters are gone, but the contents are ruined. After everything inside is gone, the walls start coming down because they are destroyed. Lastly, because there is no repair for a house in this condition, it sits in its devastated state until it eventually crumbles.

I can't let Alzheimer's kill something in me before or even if it does decide to flood me. I can't allow the sadness and depression to overcome me to the point of not being able to function and blaming it on the possibility of the plaques taking over. Depression is so consuming. It takes over your thoughts. Your stifled thoughts become anxiety and cause your heart and mind to race. You physically feel the effects of your mind's darkness. You are achy and slow and overwhelmed to the point of being frozen. It crushes who you are. Depression can be controlled with medication and lifestyle changes. It doesn't go away quickly, and for some folks, it never goes away.

I struggle with slipping quickly into depression. It has stomped me hard twice in my life. Other times, it has been a reasonably swift recovery. I pray and look for biblical solutions such as the concept of Sabbath for more precise boundaries in my life and self-care. I've tried the medication route. I couldn't function with the prescription I was given. However, it would help me calm down enough to sleep. I only took the medication a few times because I didn't like the way it made me feel. I sound like a typical non-compliant patient. Thankfully, I've been able to step out of my episodes after a short period of time.

I wanted to be real in this book and share my heart. I know that if you are beginning your journey or at the end of your time with a loved one battling Alzheimer's, you understand my feelings and fears. You stay strong to take care of the person dear to your heart, but you are dying a little inside as you watch them die. It's such a cruel disease.

I wasn't my Dad's caretaker. My mom was. I watched her deal with his episodes of confusion and obsessions and odd behaviors. One minute she acknowledged he was getting worse and the next minute she fussed that he ignored her and did his best to go against her wishes. She defended him, and she cursed him. She wanted no advice from my sister and me, but she wanted our support. Her world had been completed interrupted and turned upside down. The man she depended on for safety and security now needed to rely on her for everything. Her life was chaos, so she worked overtime to try to control every tiny detail. It was hard to watch.

I worried about her health when she would be in a rage because he had done something and wouldn't stop talking about buying a truck. It was like she was about to blow steam out the top of her head. She'd make an excuse to stop at my house unannounced, just to get out of her own. I don't blame her. She was doing the very best she was capable of doing.

The stress took a toll on her. She stopped being able to see the reality of his condition. Julie or I would mention that we would notice he was starting to slur his words or was slumping to one side in his chair. She'd quickly say, "He's fine. He just fell asleep that way and hasn't sat back up."

Nope. That's not what happened, but if you pushed the issue, she'd get mad.

She started saying, "You and your sister think you know what is going on with your Daddy. You truly have no idea. I'm the one that is here every day, 24-hours a day, with him. I think I know better than you do as to what's going on with him."

The sad thing was that her assessment of him was not as grim as was ours. Sometimes when she was exhausted, it was grim. But when she was mad and frustrated, he knew exactly what he was doing.

I've since explained to her that we had a better vantage point in seeing Daddy's quick decline in the last few months of his life. It was like seeing my grandkids once a week. I can see Connor becoming more independent and saying new words. I see Stella's legs are longer than the week before. I feel her growing stronger. The snapshots of their lives let me see new and exciting growth; whereas their parents don't notice until they have to buy new clothes because the kids had already grown out of the new ones they just bought.

I told my mom, "You can stare at a plant every day for weeks and not actually see or notice it grow until it sprouts or blooms. If I see a pot of dirt and then the next week see the tiny shoot, then I can see progress."

She was too caught up in the weeds that were choking the life out of her soulmate that she couldn't see him dying.

Although I was not his daily caretaker and companion, my pain is real, too. He was my father. He is a part of my DNA. My hands, and especially my feet, look just like his. He was a source of security and foundation for me. Why do I think he was a great dad? Because I never had to doubt that he was dependable, stable, and faithful. I never doubted that he loved me unconditionally, even when he had to correct me. I could hold his hand, and everything was okay. It was strong and stable. It gave me a sense of protection.

He always came to my rescue in the big and small things in life. When I moved back from Houston to begin my new, single life in Groves, he stepped up to tell me every move I needed to make. We butted heads many times over the first couple of weeks. Finally, we had to come to an understanding over some Dairy Queen ice cream.

"Thank you for loving me and wanting to take care of me. However, I need your support, not your orders."

"Hmmm. So, you aren't going to do what I tell you to do?"

"You don't have to tell me what to do. Please don't stop making suggestions, but no more orders."

"I'm really proud of you, and I want what is best for you. I'll try to start making suggestions, as you call them. You're going to be all right."

And I was all right. He would start to tell me what to do, then say, "That was a suggestion, not an order."

When the time came for me to help him, I would take his hand to lead him. He'd always pull away.

"I know where I'm going."

"I know you know where you're going. I'm cold, and you need to warm me up. And I like holding on to you when we are walking. You smell good."

That worked every time because he was always willing to help me. And he liked smelling good. That same sense of protection and security was there, even when our roles were reversed.

My left brain wants answers, such as Why. Not out of fear but out of precaution. Was there anything in his lifestyle and eating habits that contributed to this disease? Was it a predisposition? What can I avoid in life to prevent this death? I know it's not a guarantee, but I know I'm more likely to get run over walking in the middle of a busy highway than I am standing in the grass. A car may veer off the road and hit me, but the odds are way less. I'm what is called a risk-averse person. If I lessen the odds of a bad thing happening, then that's the way I go. It's not fear. To me, it's trying to make the best and wisest choice. I am not very good at this, but I do try.

I want to do research. My left brain wants to do polls and graphs and charts to find trends in lifestyles, eating regimens, and family medical histories. I did mention I'm an accountant, right? There's strength in numbers. There's kinship in number. There are hidden answers in numbers. There's company for our misery in numbers. I want rational and tangible answers to this irrational and intangible disease. If I can figure it out, I can fix it. That's how the rest of my life works. So why doesn't it work in this situation?

Chapter 17

Next To The Last Trip To Heaven

In May of 2017, my mom went to Galveston for the day with her best friend. It gave her a much-needed break, and it gave me an opportunity to spend the day with Daddy.

Doug and I picked him up at 6:00 a.m. Mom had him all dressed and ready, like he was a kid going to his grandma's house. He had an extra shirt, extra pull-up, his medicines, and tissues. Well, not actually tissues. He liked napkins from the deli in town, so he had several plastic gallon-sized bags full of them and stacks everywhere. Doug and I loaded him in the truck and headed to breakfast at Whataburger.

For non-Texan readers, Whataburger has the best breakfast and burgers around. I'm pretty sure their breakfast taquitos are served in heaven. My dad would eat there every morning for many years when he was still independent. He's always been a big breakfast person. Sometimes he had two breakfasts. One out at a restaurant and one at home. If you joined him, he'd buy your meal, but you had to pay the tip.

He would go to the same restaurant every single morning until he would have to move because it closed or went up a dollar on his morning ritual – pancakes, eggs, bacon, hash browns, and toast. He'd have coffee and water and put an ice cube in his coffee to cool it off. And, he always drank the coffee with his left hand, even though he was right-handed. His theory was, there were more right-handed people than left-handed people. The odds of people drinking from the coffee cup on the left side were less than the right side. So, if the person in the kitchen didn't wash dishes very well, you were less likely to get germs. I do the same thing now because the gross-out factor of his observation never wore off.

Daddy went out for breakfast around 5:30 a.m. every single morning except Sundays. I loved breakfast with him at whatever "greasy spoon," as he called it, he was frequenting. His menu changed a bit when he started going to Whataburger every day. Two pancakes, two sausage patties, a senior coffee (because it's free) and water. He would cut the pancakes and sausages into equal, small pieces. Then he would eat a bite of pancake, then a bite of sausage. He'd do that a few times, stop, count the pieces, then continue. It was quirky, and Doug loved to watch him do it. I honestly don't remember if he had always eaten like this. Doug picked up on it and pointed it out to me. Either way, it was his routine.

When I asked Doug if he would like to take Daddy to the woods, I really didn't think he would because of all the issues he had the last few times they were out there to hunt. I was somewhat surprised when he said "yes" immediately when I asked him the day before. It wasn't because Doug didn't enjoy being with my Dad. He loved my Dad. It was because caring for him had become so much more difficult. You really had to watch him because his balance wasn't steady, and he would wander off. When Doug agreed to take us to the woods, it was obvious that he was looking forward to our trip. As I thought about it, I realized Doug, and my Dad, had lots of good memories in those woods.

Doug honed his love of hunting out there. He and my dad bonded like men do over a campfire, with stories about seeing "the big one."

As we left the restaurant and headed out to the woods, I thought about all the times Daddy had made this trip. I thought of our trips together. We would drive through the early morning, stomachs full of good food and coffee, pipe smoke rising out the cracked, driver's side window, listening to his oldies tapes. I think he had every rock-n-roll song from the '50s on his tapes. He'd sing along with them and play the drums on the steering wheel. Sometimes he'd say the line before it was time, then sing it. It was a weird habit he had. And, his truck smelled like peppermint gum and pipe tobacco. Riding with him like this was one of my happy places. It felt peaceful, secure, and content.

The morning of our adventure, things didn't feel right because we weren't listening to music. Daddy's kind of music. I pulled up some of the songs he loved on my cell phone. Little Richard should get him bopping his head and maybe singing a little. But, he didn't. How about a little Chuck Berry? That didn't work either. I'd ask him if he liked whatever I was playing. He'd say "yes," but when Doug asked if he knew the name of the song, Daddy would say he didn't think he had heard it before. I was determined to find some recognition. I played every song I could think of that he loved.

Nothing.

He sat emotionless.

And then it happened. Doug stopped to get gas at a store at an intersection on the way to the camp. I turned up my volume and played Percy Sledge singing "When A Man Loves A Woman." I was sitting in the back seat of the truck, watching his face in the side mirror. I saw a slight grin, then his head started nodding. He knew the song. Doug said, "Ronnie. You know this song?" Daddy said, "Oh yeah. Sure, sure." And I think he did. He seemed to enjoy listening to it. I played it twice because I was so excited. Old Daddy was in there. I saw him. Even though he was near the end of Stage Five, I got to see a little bit of him again.

When we got to the land, I climbed into the small trailer Doug was pulling with the four-wheeler, filled with all our stuff. Daddy was sitting behind Doug on the ATV. I felt as if it had been a matter of months and not years since I had been there last. The right-of-way leading to his camp was still vividly familiar. I wondered if it was as familiar to Dad.

It was a beautiful, crisp morning. The birds and insects were singing. It was a perfect day. Daddy was the most peaceful I had seen him in a long time. He was usually a bit nervous and agitated, but not this morning. He just stood by the truck while Doug got everything ready. He stood there silently, looking around and taking it all in. He was so at peace. It took my breath away to watch him. He may have forgotten many things, but God's creation was still a part of his heart and mind.

We went to the camp-house first and unloaded the ice chest and other things we brought. He piddled around and seemed to be very alert. He would walk around, looking at different things around the camp. I'd tell him about them, and he'd say, "I know. I know." He said that because he didn't know, but he didn't like me telling him.

We spent our half-day riding around on the four-wheeler, trimming limbs from the path. Doug was driving, and Daddy and I were sharing the uncomfortable metal rack on the back. It wasn't very safe, but we were going slower than walking speed. We always laughed that Daddy never went over two miles an hour on that four-wheeler. Putt Putt Putt. I'm not sure why he went so slow. Every time Doug would gas the engine to go a little faster, my dad would huff and say, "Dern it!" I'd start laughing, and he'd scowl at me. He still didn't like going fast.

We made our way to the pond.

Back in its prime, the pond was beautiful. It was smooth and calm, filled with life. Fish, turtles, insects, and an occasional bird or two. Daddy admitted to swimming out there when he was alone. It was peace and stillness and heaven to him.

On this Saturday, we navigated the overgrown path to the pond. He became a little disoriented when we got there. The once-maintained levee was covered in small pine tree saplings and tall weeds. There was no walking around it anymore. The clear waters were now covered by small lily pads. I'm sure there was still some nice-sized bass in there, but you couldn't see them. The center of the pond was much bigger too, due to a lower water level.

The scene he had etched in his memory had drastically changed into something he didn't recognize. I must admit I was taken back, as well. The change in the pond mirrored what was happening to him. The beauty of its past glory was now covered by trees and weeds that didn't belong. Those intruders choked the life and functionality out of something that was once vibrant and useful. Where Daddy had once felt complete standing on the banks of the pond he carefully developed and cultivated, today he stood looking at something he couldn't recognize or comprehend. It didn't bring him joy as it once did. He didn't feel secure. He was confused. At that moment, I realized I felt the same way when I looked at him sometimes. I don't recognize the man inside the smiling exterior. He's not the once vibrant, useful, teeming-with-life man that brought me joy and security.

His mind has been taken over by weeds. My joy is different now. It's bittersweet now, and my security is gone.

It's unsettling when you have a vivid memory of something, and the reality is entirely different.

I was glad when we left the pond. The reality of its deterioration was a little more than I wanted to see. We hopped back on the four-wheeler, and Doug drove us out to one of his deer blinds, high up in the trees. As we stopped under the stand, we smelled it. Something was stinking up the area. Doug climbed the ladder, slowly opened the door, and looked inside. It was a baby buzzard. The little guy was still covered in white fuzz, but he was so smelly that Doug was gagging. Buzzards are nasty. Daddy and I laughed at Doug as he carried on and made barf faces. It was fun to see Daddy laugh, even if it was at Doug's expense.

As we finished our tour of the property, Doug wanted to show me a stand way out past where they usually hunted. There were no clear paths, and the trip was much bumpier. Daddy was holding on and saying "Dern it" a lot more -- and louder. I told Doug to take us back to the camp because Daddy wasn't enjoying himself anymore, but he was determined to show us this stand. After one last big bump, Daddy was ready to go. I yelled to Doug to stop, and he did, right next to a bush about as high as the seat on the four-wheeler. A huge wild hog hopped up on the other side of the bush, looked at us, and took off running away from us. I yelled at Doug, "You better get us back to the camp, right now!" I had had enough nature for the day. So had Daddy.

We went back to the camp and sat out on the porch. Of course, we had peanut butter cheese crackers and root beer. That's just what you do when you are in heaven in Sour Lake. Doug mowed around the camp, and Daddy and I watched. It was a great day and one I will cherish forever. I have pictures from that day. In them, I can see the peace on Daddy's face. It was a look I didn't see very often anymore. That land was so important to him. It was his paradise. I'm thankful I got to be there for his last trip.

Chapter 18

A Glimmer Of Hope Tarnished

In July, 2017, Daddy got a new Alzheimer's doctor when his previous doctor moved out of state. As the new doctor reviewed his medical history, he noticed Daddy had a large amount of fluid build-up showing in his original MRI from 2013. He asked if his previous doctor had pointed it out to us. We told him no. He said he wanted to do some testing for a condition called Normal Pressure Hydrocephalus. It is a neurological condition that can occur in adults fifty-five years and older. NPH is an accumulation of cerebrospinal fluid (CSF) causing the ventricles of the brain to enlarge, in turn stretching the nerve tissue of the brain, causing a triad of symptoms. The symptoms of NPH are very similar to those of Alzheimer's or Parkinson's.[12]

The doctor ordered an MRI. The newest scan showed that he still had a great deal of fluid on his brain. The doctor said that he could remove some of it. With the procedure, Daddy may see an improvement in his gait and in his bladder control. The picture on the front cover of this book is from this series of MRI images. We knew from the amount of atrophy in his brain, evidenced in the most recent images, he would probably not see improvement in his cognitive state. However, the chance of giving him a better quality of life made the procedure worth trying. If the removal of the fluid resulted in positive results, they would put in a shunt to help regulate what remained. The procedure was scheduled for September, right before his 74th birthday.

Julie and I both did some research. She remembered hearing from a client that their dad had the same procedure. She called her friend and learned that her father had some success. The friend said the results were like "night and day." There was hope for our Dad to have less hardship in his daily life. I was outwardly subdued in my hope for success, but internally, I expected a miracle. I confessed my optimism to my daughter, "This can bring my Daddy back." Although we knew it wouldn't heal him, there was an expectation that it would help him.

We arrived at the hospital and Daddy was taken for testing. They did blood work, then a physical test, and a psychological test. The young man doing his physical examination was very nice to Daddy. He'd talk directly into Dad's ear so he could hear him. He'd say, "Mr. Carlin, I need you to stand here with your heels together. Now close your eyes and count to 20." Daddy watched the attendant intently. He wanted to pass the test. He put his heels together and smiled at the man. The man would say, "Now close your eyes and count to twenty." Daddy started, "One, Two, Three, Four, Five, Six, Seven, Eight, Nine, Ten, Eleven, Twenty!" He opened his eyes and smiled at the man again. "Eleven, Twenty. That's goofy," Daddy said. The attendant said, "It's okay. Let's do it again and count all the way to 20. No cheating this time." Daddy closed his eyes and start counting again. He skipped several numbers and ended with 20.

The next test required he stand on one foot and count to ten. Daddy lifted his foot, and the young man said, "Go." Daddy started, "Uno, Dos, Tres, Ten." The man laughed.

"Good! Now let's try it again. Are you going to count in Spanish again?" Dad answered, somewhat perplexed, "No. I can't speak Spanish." It was so funny. He was enjoying himself.

After the physical testing, the psychologist asked him questions for an hour. Daddy thought he did a good job and answered them all correctly. We had mentioned to the medical staff that Daddy's nose ran all the time. He had allergies, but the drainage was much worse than it had ever been. It poured from his nose, and we were continually wiping it for him. They gave us a collection bottle to gather some of the fluid. They were going to test to see if it was spinal fluid. It was later determined that it was not.

The next morning, Julie and I were dressed and ready to go. Mom and Dad were in an adjoining room. Daddy came to sit with us while Mom finished getting everything together. Julie and I took a picture with him and posted it on Facebook. We asked for prayers for him, as we were hopeful for the day and the improvements it promised. I also took a picture of him just staring off into space. *"What is he thinking?"*

We went to the hospital and got him checked in. Julie explained to the staff that his condition caused him to fidget. He was required to be still, and that would not happen unless she stayed in the room with him. She had been an X-ray technician, so medical procedures didn't bother her in the least. They consented and let her stay with him.

As he laid on his side, she sat next to him, holding his hand. Calming him as only she could. They drained a large amount of fluid from his brain using a spinal tap. When the procedure was over, they wheeled him into a recovery area.

HE WAS

Unfortunately, the procedure didn't go as we had expected.

We were in a tiny curtained recovery room. The lights were dim. When Daddy woke up, he didn't know where he was. He wanted to use the bathroom. He demanded to stand up to go. Mom was arguing with him and telling him he had to lay flat on his back. He was not understanding and not cooperating. The nurses came in and gave Mom a urinal. He was able to go and then relaxed a bit. He dozed off. When he woke up again, he was even more confused than before. This time he held on to the side rails and tried to sit up. All three of us were talking at once, trying to get him to lie down. I moved my face in his line of sight and told him to lie down. He looked at me with no recognition. His jaw was clenched, and his teeth were gritted. He was scared. He didn't know us, and he didn't know what was happening. It was horrible. The time he spent in recovery seemed to last for hours. He would go from times of sleeping to times of fighting to sit up and get up. He was worse than when he went in. We were told it would take a couple of hours to see any positive effects. I was hoping this would go away and he would be better than he was when we arrived that morning.

We knew Alzheimer's disease eventually would take his life. We just didn't realize it was going to be sooner than later.

The man who performed his physical testing the day before came to re-test him, expecting to see positive results. As Daddy was less talkative and less able to follow directions, the young man would avoid eye contact with me as they walked up and down the halls. At one time, the man asked my Dad, "Who are those two ladies?" while pointing at my sister and me. Daddy said as he pointed at me, "That's Louise." He looked at Julie and told him, "She's the dark-haired girl."

When the physical testing was over, Daddy, Julie, and I went back into his room. Daddy was facing Julie, and I was behind her, facing the back of her head. Daddy put his hands on her shoulders and moved her out of the way so he could see me.

He said, "Who is that dark-haired girl?"

Julie moved back into his line of sight and said, "You talking about me?"

"Yes." He then moved her out of the way again so he could see me.

She popped back up and said, "I'm Julie. I'm your daughter."

"Really? What's your last name?"

"Sanders. But it used to be Carlin."

"Hmm. Okay."

He became a little more aware as the day progressed, and he figured out who we were again. Thank goodness.

The days at the hospital were surreal. I didn't realize that the way he talked and told stories and moved about was so noticeably impaired until I saw the sad looks on the attendants' and nurses' faces. They would look at us like, *"I'm so sorry he's so sick."* I guess it had been such a slow, daily progression that we didn't notice how far he had regressed. At the hospital, we saw him out of his element. He was nervous and out of his comfort zone rather than at home in his recliner. Normally, when Daddy was nervous,

Julie would sit next to him and show him funny animal videos and make him laugh. But today he was nervous, quiet, scared, and not easily calmed. Julie laid in the bed with him and held his hand while they watched videos and television. My mother's anxiety and fear of the situation came out differently. She tried to act like it wasn't bad by being overly happy and cheerful. That's just how she deals with it. But I couldn't deal with any of it. I had to keep leaving the room. I couldn't deal with the circus that was going on with my mom being super happy and cheerful and my dad saying "What?" It was chaos. It was the worst kind of chaos. It was mentally-disabled confusion. I would step away and work. I would walk over to the elevator banks where they had a gurney and sit on it and answer emails or make phone calls for work. I just needed to disappear and concentrate on something that was not Alzheimer's. I'd go find coffee or go to the bathroom in the hallway or just stand in a remote hallway. I just couldn't be in that room. The air was stifling.

Fortunately, my daughter lived close to the hospital, and my sister and I were able to escape and have dinner with her for the two nights we were there. I needed to get away. I needed peace and quiet. This turn of events was so devastating. I remember thinking how draining this time was to my body and spirit. I then thought about the reason we were in this hospital. As the excess spinal fluid was removed from his brain, his life drained from his body.

The man who made the trip to Houston moved solidly into Stage Six during those few days. They were the beginning of his final days. The follow-up visit with the doctor was grim. The doctor seemed shocked at how diminished Daddy had become. As we sat in his office, he put two MRI scans up onto the lighted display. Both had what looked like a brain and red patches on them. The one on the left had several large red areas. The one on the right had a few, small round spots. The doctor explained that red represented blood flow. The image on the left was before the procedure, and the image on the right was after. I asked the doctor, "Now which one was from before and which one was after?" He would point. The left was before. The right was after. I asked the same question over and over again, in different ways, looking for a different answer. My mind couldn't comprehend that the man sitting two people down from me, talking about being a medic in the Army reserve and mixing it with another unrelated story, was functioning with so little blood flow to his brain. I also realized at that moment that the minimal blood flow meant limited time left.

I pushed the doctor to tell me how long Daddy had left. He was such a nice man, and I could tell he didn't want to say. He finally, quietly said, "About a year."

Chapter 19

New People In The House

Shortly after he came home from Houston, Daddy began declining quickly. He developed a urinary tract infection and ended up in the emergency room. We thought he was going to die. He couldn't walk or talk. Mom had to call the ambulance to get him to the hospital.

It was time for mom to get help. Julie and I sat with Mom and the representative from home health. They would send people to bathe him, give him physical therapy, and to assess him physically. He liked the man who would do his physical therapy. They walked around the house and yard and talked.

One thing he did not like was that a stranger now gave him a bath. After the first time, my mom asked him if everything went okay and he said yes. But I could tell he was nervous and upset about something. He just couldn't verbalize what it was. I spent some time making small talk with him in his bedroom. I pulled up the shower chair and sat on it while he sat on the bed. He looked at me and frowned. After an hour of talking and listening to what he was trying to say, I finally understood. These days he spoke in puzzle pieces, descriptions rather than direct. He was uncomfortable with the nurse cleaning his private area. He had been with the same woman his entire life. Now some other woman is performing a very private and intimate task for him. He got upset when I finally said, "You don't like that lady washing your business do you?" He said, "No! No! No!" He looked ashamed and sad. How degrading and undignified for him. I told him it was okay to put a towel over himself and let her know that he would take care of his own business. He seemed a little bit relieved, but then he asked me a couple of times again about it. I reassured him each time, "You tell that lady that you are going to wash your own business." I made sure Mom knew and that she would tell the attendant. I told her several times, so she wouldn't forget to tell them. He was embarrassed and helpless.

At the first of April, 2018, we realized it was time to move on to hospice. We were expecting he would be on it for at least six months. The good thing about hospice is that they would oversee his medical care. They provided diapers and a wheelchair and anything else he needed. They took over his bathing and provided his medication. They also had my mother execute a "Do Not Resuscitate" order for him. We knew that when the time came for him to go, they would keep him comfortable and be there for us. We were preparing for something we thought would be a long time in the future.

We contacted a friend who worked for a local hospice company. While we were talking to him, Roger, the gentleman who mows my parents' yard, was finishing up his job. My Dad was in the den watching television with Doug. He got up and walked to the back bedroom. Doug assumed to go to the on-suite bathroom. Mom looked up and saw Daddy in the front yard hugging Roger. He had gone out to pay him, although Mom had already paid him. He came back in, and we introduced him to our friend, Darin. He gave Darin a firm handshake and asked what happened to his hair. Darin keeps his head shaved and Daddy, as usual, pointed out that he had the most hair.

HE WAS

We didn't know if Daddy would qualify for hospice. We are glad he did because we did not know we would need it so soon.

Chapter 20

All The Daddies I Loved

Darin called him feeble. That word means weak, frail, and fragile. My mind immediately shouted, "*He's not feeble! He still has a strong handshake and could hurt you if he gave you a right-hook to the stomach.*"

But he was right. Daddy was feeble. He walked like the old man portrayed by Tim Conway on The Carol Burnett Show.

Shuffle, Shuffle.
Stop and look around.
Then shuffle a little farther.
Repeat.

He didn't stand up well from a sitting position, and he had a difficult time sitting down. He was pale. He was slow. He was somewhat disheveled, but not a mess.

That is who he was now.

As I reflected on this, looking back through time at where we had come from and how the drastic changes happened before my eyes, I remembered that I didn't seem to notice them until they were long past.

I felt like my Dad had died about six times already. Several years ago, as I mentioned earlier, many events led up to "the talk." We knew we thought he had issues but didn't have verification. He went to the doctor, and the doctor said, "*You have Alzheimer's disease.*"

I mourned the death of Daddy Number One. He's the dad who raised me. He's the dad who gave me advice, discussed accounting problems with me, and helped me talk through all kinds of issues. Daddy Number One drove me through torrential rainstorms to pick up my daughter on Sunday afternoons because I was afraid to drive in the rain. Daddy Number One was smart and strong and invincible. Daddy Number One had been fading away and became Daddy Number Two before any of us knew what was happening.

Daddy Number Two was a lot like Daddy Number One, and sometimes you couldn't tell them apart. He was friendly and talkative. He looked the same and laughed the same. He knew everyone he saw regularly. He knew some folks as someone he should know but wasn't sure how he knew them. But he smiled and talked to them anyway. Daddy Number Two was very frustrated. He couldn't drive anymore, and he HATED IT! But he still worked in the yard, hugged me tightly and offered to help Julie and me any time we needed anything. Daddy Number Two poured all his energy and intelligence into proving he didn't have Alzheimer's. He was scared and mad. Rightly so. We were, too.

His educational packets for the doctor got thinner and thinner over the next couple of years. The last package he brought was just papers he found on his desk. He knew he brought his portfolio to appointments but didn't remember what documents he carried in it. I remember that appointment. Daddy Number Two had become Daddy Number Three, and I had missed it. When did he lose his creative and curious mind? He was moving slower and becoming more cantankerous with my mom. But I guess, just like before, I chose to not see the decline.

Daddy Number Three wears diapers. He puts his fake tooth in his contact case. He really shuffles now. He wants a new yellow truck like the one we made him sell. That one was blue, but there is no convincing him. He remembers a yellow truck. He wants to go hunting. No one will take him. He knows the pretty girls at the dinner table are our family and his grandkids, but he doesn't always remember who they belong to. He still loves them and lights up around them. We put a towel on his chair during dinner. And, he's forgotten how he would save a piece of meat to eat with his dessert. He still remembers how much he loves sweets and ice cream. Daddy Number Three stopped bringing information to the doctor appointments. He introduced himself to the doctor the last time we were there.

Daddy Number Three became Daddy Number Four in mid-September, 2017 when he had a procedure to drain excess fluid from his brain. What should have been the means to him walking better and having better control of his bladder resulted in the complete opposite. The procedure killed Daddy Number Three. Daddy Number Four woke up in his place, and he didn't know us. He was scared and combative. He clenched his jaw and tensed his muscles. Daddy Number Four got a little less stressed throughout his hospital stay, but Daddy Number Three never came back. This was my new Daddy. We had a new reality, again.

Before he left the hospital, he knew who we were, but it was like Daddy Number Three had jumped off a cliff, died and Daddy Number Four was the victim that got up off the valley floor and tried to keep going.

Shortly after the procedure, he developed a severe urinary tract infection, I'm assuming from the fluid pills he was now on to prevent additional spinal fluid accumulation. It was scary. He couldn't walk or talk. The ambulance had to transport him to the hospital. He received treatment and was discharged. Daddy Number Five came home from the ER. He was more like Daddy Number Four and a half at first, but he quickly moved to Daddy Number Five.

Over the next several months, Daddy Number Six arrived. His body was shutting down. His appetite was disappearing, and it could take him over an hour to eat half of a sandwich. He no longer stood to hug and kiss when I came in the door. He still bugged my mom to take him to get a new truck, but he was easily redirected to another subject. He didn't mess around in his office anymore. He slept a lot.

Daddy Number Seven was who came next. He was the last version of my Dad here on earth.

Chapter 21

Moving To Rose Street

After just a week or so with hospice coming to their home, mom expressed that it was time to meet with a private care home. Dad had started slumping over in his chair, and his face seemed to droop on one side. Mom said he had just been sleeping and didn't sit back up. I knew that wasn't the case. My sister and I figured he had a stroke. Because of his weakened state, Mom couldn't physically take care of Daddy anymore. We weren't surprised, because he wasn't able to help her care for himself anymore.

On Monday I called and made an appointment for Wednesday with Penny, the owner of a private care home. We had met her through the daughter of one of her residents. We knew a few other of her residents, too. Mom, Julie, and I showed up and liked her immediately. We went to the house and saw where his room would be. Penny asked about his medications and about his routines. She wanted to know his favorite shows and favorite foods. She wanted to make his experience at her home as comfortable and inviting as being in his own home.

One of the residents was a friend from our church. His mind was pretty good during the day, but he would sundown at night. Physically his wife could no longer take care of him. I sat next to him and visited for a moment. I asked him if he liked it there. He looked at me so sadly, dropped his head, and shook it no.

"Are you telling me you don't like it here or would you rather be at home?"

"I want to go home with Beverly."

"If you can't go home, is this a good place to be instead?"

He kept his head and eyes down and said, "Yes."

"I heard the food here is really good."

He looked up at me with a sparkle in his eyes and said, "Yeah. It's really good. I wish Penny would teach Beverly how to make fried eggs."

I needed to talk to him a little bit because I needed to know that these were good people and a good place for my Dad to live for the remainder of his life. I know he would have told me if it wasn't. Mainly because of his strong desire to go home.

We arranged for Penny to come to Mom and Dad's house. She was going to bring cookies and visit him in his own environment. She wanted to spend some time visiting with the four of us in his comfort zone. It was her way of observing our family dynamic and how we all worked together. It was a real opportunity for her to see Dad at his most relaxed, comfortable state. She could see who he really was and what to expect from him. Knowing these things would let her know when he was out of sorts and not himself. She's incredible at what she does. She cares deeply about the individuals she brings to live in her home.

When I arrived at Mom and Dad's on Friday, Penny and Julie were already there. I had stopped by someone's office at work to drop off some paperwork before I headed that direction and got the best little gift. Earlier in the day, our intellectual and developmental disabilities program had a butterfly release. They would each talk about the loss of people and other things in their lives. Then, they would open the tiny paper envelope in their hands and release the beautiful butterfly inside. It was symbolic of releasing the sadness. There had been extra butterflies, and I got one. I knew Daddy would love the butterfly release. He loved all things in nature.

I walked in the den, and he was sitting, leaning, in his recliner. The effects from the stroke were pretty pronounced today, almost like he had had another smaller one.

Penny visited and then invited us over for lunch the next day. She told Daddy she was going to fix dinner for him. He didn't know he wouldn't be coming home after lunch. After our visit, we all walked Penny to the front door. Daddy couldn't walk. His right side was weak, and his leg wasn't cooperating. Neil and Doug had arrived, so they helped him to the front porch. I showed him the envelope and told him to watch closely. As I opened it, he saw the butterfly. "It's a bug," he said. I said, "It's a butterfly. Let's set him free and watch him fly away." And that's what we did. Daddy watched the butterfly take flight. He said, "Oops" and then laughed. I knew he'd love it.

After Penny left, Daddy needed to be cleaned up. He and mom went into the hall bathroom. He had to stand up so Mom could clean him. She kept telling him to stand up, and it was not happening. It was emotional for them both and for us hearing it. It was awful listening to the struggle. When he came out, he was shaky and sweaty and gasping for air. He was looking at me with fear in his eyes as he gasped for air. He looked like a fish out of water. As he struggled to breathe, his eyes would bulge. My heart hurt so bad that I could barely breathe myself. We got him in the recliner and hooked him up to some oxygen. After several minutes, his breathing was better, and he was more relaxed.

That evening, Julie and I got pictures off the wall in his office, and mom packed a suitcase of clothes. We were moving him to Rose Street. It was a perfect street name for him, since he loved roses. Julie and I went to his new home and decorated it with pictures of him and his brothers, pictures of him fishing and hunting and photographs of his wife and family. We wanted him to feel us all around him and to see familiar things in this strange place. We brought his CPA certificate because we knew how proud he was of that accomplishment. As we decorated the walls with things he loved, my heart was so heavy. I knew he would die at this place. In this room. I wanted it to be the most loving, joy-filled room he had ever been in, so that he could be at peace without a shadow of a doubt about how much he was loved.

I didn't sleep much Friday night. I prayed for the Lord to take him before we had to move him, so I waited for a call early Saturday. It didn't come. I guess I was relieved, but I was anxious for the day.

We told mom that we would wait until she called for us to come because we knew that she had lots of things to get ready. She also had to get him ready, and they didn't move very fast in the morning. At 11:00 a.m. mom called me. I had been dressed and playing a game online, so I didn't have to think about life. When I walked in the back door, she was all abuzz, flailing and yelling in a nervous tizzy. She would say she needed help and then would say, "Don't touch that." She was not in a good place. Dad was in the bathroom, and she was about to brush his teeth. Julie came in, and we were trying to pick up some things he might need, but Mom was not having it. She told us to let her go brush his teeth. This required him to stand up at the sink. Mom is five-foot-tall, and he was six-foot-two. Although she acted like she was strong, she was not physically capable of holding him up. It took quite some time, but she got his teeth brushed and moved him to the bed. My sister and I walked in there, and he was sweating like someone had doused him with water. He was so out of breath that he was gasping for air like he did the day before. This time, we moved him to the shower chair in their bedroom. Mom plugged in the oxygen tank and gave him some relief. He couldn't hold himself up to sit straight, so I knelt beside him and looked up at his face.

I said, "I love you. Do you know that?"

"Yeah. Why?" He laughed.

I stroked his sweat-soaked hair out of his face.

"Don't do that. You're messing up my hair."

"Your hair is already messy. I'm trying to help."

"Your hair is a mess, too."

It was. He always told me to brush my unruly hair. It was a sweet moment as we just looked into each other's eyes while he tried to breathe. Unbeknownst to him, Julie and Neil were in the den moving his recliner out the front door to their truck. They wanted it to be at Penny's before we arrived.

When Mom was done, Julie, Mom, and I got him to his feet and helped him to the car. Because his weakness was so prevalent now, it was a long and painful process trying to get him down the back stairs. We packed the wheelchair provided by hospice. We couldn't leave yet, because Julie and Neil needed time to get the chair in place at his new home. As we sat there, I tried to make him smile. He wasn't smiling. The last time I saw him smile was at the butterfly. I think he was so exhausted and weak.

Julie called and told us to come, and so we did. We got to Penny's and put him in the wheelchair. Julie had made some cookies and put them in a container for him to give to Penny. She also brought some of his Double Delight roses in a blue cup for her.

Penny greeted us at the door and introduced him to everyone. We wheeled him to his place at the table, and she served him a plate of roast, rice, and gravy. A true southern meal. He didn't want to eat. He would look at all the people there, one at a time, then stare into my eyes blankly. He would look around again then stare at me.

He knew. He didn't say anything, but he knew.

Penny saw he wasn't eating so she asked if he wanted some ice cream. That perked him up, and he said yes. Julie sat next to him and began feeding him one bite of roast, then one bite of ice cream. It sounds weird, but he always liked mixing dinner and dessert.

We stayed for most of the day. Mom left first, then Julie, then Doug and me. I didn't want him to feel abandoned, but he was. It was what was best for him, but that did not make it any easier. I didn't sleep that night. I didn't sleep for the five nights he was there. I'd visit him and watch television with him and help him eat. I have no words for what I felt other than sadness. Dark, heart-wrenching sadness covered in a smile so he wouldn't be sad. But he was. He was very sad. He was quiet and didn't ask to go home.

On Wednesday, I left work early. I was going to Austin for a work conference, and I did not want to go. I felt that something was going to happen, and I needed to be close to home. Doug and I went to visit Daddy before I left. We visited, and I fed him his dinner. I also fed him the banana pudding Julie had brought him the day before. He loved sweets and enjoyed every bite. His breathing was very labored. His hands and feet were ice-cold, and he was sweating, but the rest of his body was normal temperature. His legs were splotchy like he was cold. The droop of his face was more pronounced, and he was drooling a little. The hospice nurse suspected a urinary tract infection and was going to give him an antibiotic. I told Penny I was going to cancel my trip to Austin, but she said she didn't think anything was imminent and I should go. They would call me if things changed. The hospice nurse agreed with her.

I just knew in my heart that I shouldn't go. I told him I was going to Austin and I would be back the next evening. We hugged and kissed each other's cheeks several times. I told him I loved him, and he told me he loved me. I walked away and told him goodbye. I hesitated at the front door. I turned around to see him one more time, but I couldn't see him from where I stood. I turned back around and left.

My drive to Austin was excruciating. I normally love the drive because it is pretty, and I can listen to music. But this evening was different. I never turned on the radio. I didn't notice the wildflowers or pastures. I stayed lost in thought. It was a long drive.

The next morning, I had breakfast with a few colleagues and found my place in the meeting room. The meeting started at 8:00 a.m. At 9:30 a.m. Julie called. I walked out to answer, and she said, "Come home. Come home now. Do not wait." I asked if he was still alive and she said he was unconscious. It seemed he had a stroke that morning while being dressed. I started shaking. I went to my room, threw my things in the suitcase and headed to the front desk to check out. I had to wait for the front-desk clerk, and it

HE WAS

seemed like an eternity. I noticed a lady from our conference in the lobby at the same time I realized I still had on my name tag. I walked over to her and asked her to put my tag back on the sign-in table. She asked me if I was okay and I said, "I have to get home before my Daddy dies."

I got in the car and called Julie. She had been up in East Texas taking care of some business. She was driving with her flashers on, trying to get to him. I got off the phone and called Doug, my daughter, Lauren, and my cousin, Cristi. Then I set my mind to the task of safely and quickly making it home before he left for heaven. I drove 90 miles an hour with my flashers on. No radio but lots of noise in my head. *"He'll never talk to me again? I talked to him yesterday. How can this be real?"* I prayed that God would let me tell him I loved him one more time. I prayed that his last moments would be peaceful. I prayed for calm and peace for myself as well. God gave me the peace that surpasses all understanding. It was an assurance of His love for both me and Daddy.

Chapter 22

He's Gone

I walked up to his bedside and placed my hands on either side of his head. I put my face on his, cheek to cheek. I felt his skin and his hair. It was familiar and comforting. I let myself relax into this hug of sorts. I whispered in his ear, "I'm here, Daddy. This is Denise. I'm here."

"I love you so much, and you have been the best Daddy I could have ever had. I love you, and it's okay to go. We will be okay, but I'm going to miss you so much."

My heart was in my throat, and I felt nauseated. I was trembling and silently crying.

I didn't want to let go. I told him, "Lauren is on her way and will be here soon. I love you, Daddy."

I sat up and got my first real sense of what was happening. Julie said he was very fitful that morning, his arms and legs twitching and moving around, as if his body were fighting to keep his spirit. He would take a deep breath, lie silently for several seconds and then exhale with a painful, mournful moan. It sounded like death. My mom was talking about sandwiches and other things. Neil said something, but I couldn't focus on anything but my Dad. Doug rubbed my back as I held Daddy's hand. I held it in a way such that I had two fingers on his pulse. If he had a pulse, I knew he was going to breathe again. I counted fourteen seconds between the inhales and the loud, horrible exhales.

Mom pulled out the paperwork hospice gave her to explain the processes his body was going through to die. I didn't want to know. I wanted to stare at him and etch his face into my mind one last time. I sat there, taking his pulse and watching his face and hating the exhales for about 45 minutes.

A text from Lauren broke my concentration. I told him Lauren had just arrived and Doug and I headed out to see her. She was standing outside her car talking with her mother-in-law. Lauren put her phone on speaker, and her mother-in-law prayed for the three of us and the rest of the family. I warned Lauren how bad it was inside. She was scared as she walked in and I honestly don't remember what she did when she got there. I do remember taking my seat back at his side, holding his hand and feeling his pulse. His heart was strong. I could feel the beats, and they were steady, unlike his breathing.

The hospice chaplain who had been with us for a while asked if he could read a scripture before he left. I walked out into the hall to be with Lauren as he read. He said, "This is the 23rd Psalm from the Passion Translation[13], and read:"

> *The Lord is my best friend and my shepherd.*
> *I always have more than enough.*
> *He offers a resting place for me in his luxurious love.*
> *His tracks take me to an oasis of peace, the quiet brook of bliss.*
> *That's where he restores and revives my life.*
> *He opens before me pathways to God's pleasure*
> *and leads me along in his footsteps of righteousness*
> *so that I can bring honor to his name.*
> *Lord, even when your path takes me through*
> *the valley of deepest darkness,*
> *fear will never conquer me, for you already have!*

You remain close to me and lead me through it all the way.
Your authority is my strength and my peace.
The comfort of your love takes away my fear.
I'll never be lonely, for you are near.
You become my delicious feast
even when my enemies dare to fight.
You anoint me with the fragrance of your Holy Spirit;
you give me all I can drink of you until my heart overflows.
So why would I fear the future?
For your goodness and love pursue me all the days of my life.
Then afterward, when my life is through,
I'll return to your glorious presence to be forever with you!

Lauren broke down, and she and I hugged tightly and cried. Suddenly, Julie said, "His eyes are open!" Daddy had opened his eyes and looked around a bit before closing them again. I walked back into the room while Julie was hurriedly moistening his mouth. Foamy saliva was building up. She kept saying, "His eyes were open!" I was broken that I missed seeing his beautiful, bright blue eyes, one more time.

I stepped to the end of the bed at his feet. Mom was now at his side. I uncovered his feet and put my hand over the top with my two fingers, feeling his pulse near his ankle. He took a breath, inhaling quickly. About 14 seconds later, he exhaled, moaning, but it stopped abruptly. It didn't fully exhale. It caught in the middle. There was a bit of foamy saliva that stuck just at the top of his tongue. We all stared and waited from the next inhale. I think we all knew there would not be another. This was it. I finally noticed his pulse had ended. The others were talking amongst themselves as to whether that was his last breath or not. It was. I knew because I had felt his last heartbeat. I told them that he no longer had a pulse. We all breathed a little shallower.

He was gone.

HE WAS

We started moving around the room, and somehow Penny knew and came in. She had something that tested his blood pressure or pulse. She said nothing was registering. His last breath on earth was at 3:15 p.m., April 26, 2018. People were called to come in. The hospice nurse, the police, the funeral home. I took my place back by his side, but not until I held his head again, burying my face into the side of his head and cheek. I told him, "Goodbye, Daddy. I am going to miss you so much."

I sat by his side, holding his now lifeless hand, rubbing my thumb across his hair and his fingers. I studied them. They looked like mine when my nails are short and unpolished. I held on and never wanted to let go. I wanted him to feel safe, although he had already left. Lauren said that shortly after he died, we all were having conversations about things other than him. She looked at him and realized, "Grandpa just saw Jesus." We were going on with life and missing the magnitude of that moment.

He Saw Jesus!

I called my step-sons, Logan and Dylan, and told them. I called my Dad's brothers, and our pastor. It was somewhat of a blur, but with sharp details. I guess it was just unreal.

The funeral home showed up an hour or so after he had been gone. I had to let go. It was the worst thing I had to do. I would never, ever hold his strong, comforting, stable hand again. They pulled up the stretcher next to the bed, positioned him in the heavy, blue body bag, and zipped it up. This can't be real. I wasn't hysterical. I wasn't complacent. I was numb.

They put the body bag with him inside onto the stretcher and wheeled him to the funeral home vehicle. Now what? I felt that "before a tragedy/after a tragedy" defining moment we all have experienced. Mine was before he died and after he died. I was standing in the gap between my old life and my new life. One changed because of his life.

Mom went home. She was tired and just wanted to go home and would find something to eat. Doug, Julie, Lauren, and I went somewhere to eat. Neil had gone to pick up their daughter, Olivia. She was flying in from Tulsa and didn't know her Grandpa had passed. They wanted to tell her in person. It felt so surreal making dinner plans. Is it okay if we eat? Do we pretend this didn't just happen?

Chapter 23

Saying Goodbye

The next day, Friday, we had to plan a funeral. My dad was not a boring, solemn guy. He was fun and full of life. He was so many things. His funeral needed to remind people of the Ronnie they knew and loved. Not the Ronnie they saw the last few years. We started off the morning at Mom's looking for pictures. We pulled some great ones of him when he was little. We found pictures from when they were dating. There was one where he had on a leather jacket and a bowtie. He was bending down on one knee in the snow and had a smirky smile like he was trying to be cool. It turned out that he and mom were broken up. PaPaw picked Mom up and brought her to the grocery store where Daddy worked. He wasn't happy to see her, and he was mad at his dad for bringing her up there. I thought it was funny because it really was a great picture of him. We gathered all the photos, and I got all his oldies music out of his desk. Julie and I wanted his oldies music playing during the visitation. He loved those songs. Mom thought it was a bit sacrilegious and inappropriate, but she let us do it anyway. She knew he would have played them if he had planned his own funeral.

We went to the funeral home. Mom and Daddy had already picked out their coffins and had started paying on them a few years prior. The reality of death hit them when my cousin succumbed to a brain aneurysm at 52 years old.

The funeral director started writing the obituary. He was a very nice and respectful guy. But he typed so slow! He kept having to correct spelling and retype things. I was coming out of my skin. Doug finally said, "Hey. Do you want Denise to type that for you? She's really fast." It was funny. The man said, "Sure. If you want to." He moved out of the way and let me sit down. I laughed and thanked him. Patience was not my biggest virtue at that moment.

His obituary was written by Mom, Julie, Lauren, Doug, and me with the intent of reminding people just who he was.

Lauren left and went to Lamar University to take her final exam for her Master of Business Administration degree. It was so emotional for her, but she knew she had to be strong and finish. Grandpa would have been so incredibly proud of her. Mom, Julie, and I dropped Doug off at home and went to the church to see Bro. Joe. We gave him Daddy's bible to flip through as he prepared the service. Since he's been our pastor and friend for years, we knew he would do an excellent service.

Mom, Julie, and I then went to the cemetery. Again, their plots had been chosen, and payments were being made. Their plot is near Daddy's mom and dad, his grandmother, his brother, aunts, uncles, and cousins. He was going to be among family. It was comforting and weird to stand in one place and know they were all there. The lady at the cemetery was showing Mom headstone options. It really wasn't the best time for it. She really wasn't in the frame of mind to choose between military emblems and quotes.

They then took us out to show us his plot. I hated it. This cemetery is beautiful and has lots of trees. There had been a large tree near his mom and dad until one of the hurricanes blew it over. He didn't have any shade. Julie said it didn't matter because he wasn't here. But it mattered to me. I wanted him comfortable. It's hard to reconcile that his body isn't him. That the person you loved was a spirit with a soul that lived in the body that had double-crossed him and let him down. His body was once the vessel that held the sweet spirit. I wanted it comfortable.

We left and had lunch and then dropped Mom off at home. People had started to drop off food. She was going to stay home and eat some roast that had been delivered by a friend. That's such a great tradition. Feeding the feelings of your friends.

Julie and I went to a local Mexican restaurant to write his eulogy. We were going to brag on our Daddy one more time. Over water, chips, salsa, and guacamole, we made a list of all the things he was to us. There was no rhyme or reason to the list. It was just our feelings. It was a good list, and it happened quickly. It helps to have a good subject. That evening, I went home and started putting together the music. His CDs were old and scratchy, so I downloaded them to a playlist named, "Funeral Songs." Who would have ever thought the song *Let The Good Times Roll* would be on a funeral song playlist?

This process went late into the night. When I finished with his oldies, I downloaded two more songs for the actual funeral, *How Great Thou Art*, the Carrie Underwood version, and *Alpha and Omega* by The Gathiers. The first song was for me. Carrie sings like an angel, and the song declares God's majesty. He was in control, and He loved my Daddy.

He was still taking care of him. *Alpha and Omega* was one of my Dad's favorites. He would play it loudly in his truck and sing happily, shaking his finger pointed to heaven. "*He is the Alpha and Omega.*" Daddy loved that truth. When the music was completed, I worked on the eulogy, categorizing the statements into "He Was" statements. He was a Godly Man. He was Smart, etcetera. Then I took the things we wrote over chips and salsa and put them in order. I marked places for us to stop and ad-lib a story about him. He would be honored in front of his friends and family tomorrow. He would have laughed at the oldies music and would have sung along. He would have been so proud of Julie and me. We wanted to make him proud. We wanted our last time with him to be special. And it was.

Visitation time was filled with so many people from our past and present. There were friends from his childhood, from his old job at the energy company, from church, from a lifetime of relationships. Mom, Julie, and I had people there who didn't know him but knew us and wanted to show their support and sympathy. It was good for my aching soul to see and hug so many people.

When the funeral began, Brother Charles, our associate pastor who was performing the service along with Brother Joe, read the 23rd Psalm that was read before his died. Then *How Great Thou Art* ushered in a time of worship. As the last note pierced the air in the room, Brother Charles introduced Julie and me. We approached the pulpit to eulogize our Dad before the packed room of witnesses.

We took a deep breath and began our declaration of love. Julie and I took turns reading and telling the stories.

Chapter 24

He Was

DENISE

Did you all hear about the time Boudreaux called the doctor because Marie went into labor?

We knew Daddy's disease had progressed when he said, "No. What happened?"

Daddy fought his way through Alzheimer's for six years. His struggles were many, yet he always remained loving to his family and enjoyed life. Even the day before he died, the nurse asked how he was doing, and he answered, "Super Great!" That was always his answer. Alzheimer's was his battle, but it was not who He Was. We want to rewind time a bit to honor him by telling you who we knew him to be.

Our Daddy was smart!

He put himself through college and earned his bachelor's degree in accounting. In 1974, with a wife, two kids and a full-time job, he got his master's in business administration from Lamar University. When he was 49 years old, after many years of studying and testing, he became a Certified Public Accountant. This is a huge accomplishment; one he had pursued and accomplished with diligence and hard work. He helped the City of Groves with their franchise taxes for free. He helped the church on the finance committee and did an internal audit. He was a Rotarian.

JULIE

I'm in Rotary with several people who were in Rotary with Dad. I asked one of Dad's old friends if Daddy ever did any of the programs. He said, "Yes! He always had great programs. One time he brought a meter from work and taught us how to steal electricity."

This got a big laugh. Especially from his old work friends.

He taught many students at Lamar State College Port Arthur how to debit the window and credit the door.

DENISE

When I went back to college in 2000, I took a second-semester accounting class. I asked the young man next to me if he had the teacher of this class for the first class. He said, "No. I had Mr. Carlin in Port Arthur. He's the best. Everyone gets an A because he's really easy to understand." A few other students chimed in and said, "Oh yeah, he's the best." I told them that he was my Dad. I was so proud of him.

Our Daddy was a Man's Man!

He loved being outside working. He spent many years researching deeds, purchasing land, then improving the land and digging a pond out in Sour Lake. He built his dream place he named, "Carlin's Killin' Time Ranch." He loved spending time with his sons-in-law out at the land. He would fish and hunt every weekend. He putt-putted around that 97 acres on his four-wheeler and admired God's creation.

He could grow roses like no-one else. They were beautiful and smelled amazing. He would cut them and share with us, the ladies at Bruce's and Subway, and anyone else who asked.

JULIE

When we went to Penny's for lunch on the day we moved him in, I cut some of his roses for him to bring to her. He liked the idea because he always liked sharing his roses. She put them on the kitchen table so everyone could smell them.

Our Daddy was a Godly Man!

He made it so easy for us both to truly understand God as a loving Father. He was a servant and always willing to help.

He was always offering to help. Even when he couldn't physically help any more, he offered anyway. I was at his house helping him clean up his rose bushes and the yard. I'd pick up something big, and he'd say, "Put that down. It's too heavy." He didn't want me carrying heavy stuff. That was a man's job, in his mind. I gave him a couple of sticks and asked him to help me carry them to the front yard. He did. It gave him that sense of helping that he desired so much. He was being useful, which was so important to him.

DENISE

He loved the Lord with all his heart. He prayed for us and shared scriptures and lessons with us. He lived his life as a Godly example. He was Honest. He was Faithful. He was Kind. He was a good provider, working hard for our family. He was a faithful, loving husband. He cared for his parents even when it was not easy.

JULIE

He would drive past our PaPaw's house early every morning on the way to breakfast to pick up his newspaper and put it at their door, so he wouldn't have to walk down the driveway to get it.

DENISE

Our Dad would want you to know the Lord as your Savior as he knew Him so well. He would want to see you in glory with him someday.

Glenn, one of the pallbearers, told me that he and his wife were talking about people who had influenced their lives. He said, "Mr. Carlin. He didn't play. We had to behave, and he would teach us about the Lord."

JULIE
Our Daddy was a Worthy Role Model!

He was consistent our entire lives. We always knew he would be coming home, and he would be happy to see us. He was reliable. You could always count on him. His word was ironclad. He was our fierce protector. He wanted us safe. If you ever tried to date one of us, you understand. He was security to us. We felt safe when he was around. Just holding his hand would bring comfort in times of trouble.

I remember one time when we were kids, Denise and I were playing outside. Denise fell in an ant bed. And, I may or may not have pushed her. Daddy came running outside, scooped her up, and ran inside to put her in the tub, rinsing off the ants.

DENISE

I hated driving in the rain. I once hydroplaned down the Veteran's Memorial Bridge in the rain. After that, I was petrified to drive in a storm. Daddy would drive me to drop-off Lauren to her Dad in Baytown and take me to pick her up. I loved these times together. We talked about all kinds of things – life, work, God. I created my business plan, and he named my company Business Enhancements. I felt secure with him at the wheel.

He worked hard and was never lazy. He never missed work. He was a planner and very detailed. He always was a sharp dresser. Unless he was working outside, his hair and clothes were always in place. And he smelled so good.

When we were kids, I thought we were rich. Most kids' dads wore Nomex and worked shift-work at the refineries. My dad wore a suit, had shiny shoes, and perfect hair. And he smelled good. I was proud of him because he looked important.

He was kind and generous to people. He was respected and respectful. He was so, so proud of us and he always told us so.

JULIE

In the end, he knew who we were and could still read. He said, *"Thank you, Shug"* and ate ice cream. Although he had been unconscious for several hours, he seemed to have waited for Denise, who had been in Austin earlier that day, to arrive. The chaplain read Psalm 23 from the Passion Translation that Bro. Charles just read.

After the final verse –

So why would I fear the future?
For your goodness and love pursue me all the days of my life.
Then afterward, when my life is through,
I'll return to your glorious presence to be forever with you!

He returned to God's glorious presence to be forever with Him.

DENISE

Our Dad loved life. He loved to laugh. He'd laugh so hard that he'd start coughing and crying and laughing at the same time. He'd turn bright red and enjoyed the whole thing. He loved dancing with Mom, and loved good oldies rock-n-roll. He loved telling the story of her catching his eye for the first time when she was five years old and three foot nothing, wearing a blue and white polka-dotted dress at the First Baptist Church. He loved working in the yard and told the Alzheimer's doctor that growing roses was his hobby and favorite pastime.

JULIE
He loved fishing, hunting, and fiddle-farting in Sour Lake. He loved a root beer and peanut-butter cheese crackers after a long morning of surveying his land. He loved Sanford and Son and M.A.S.H. I guess he finally got to join Fred & Elizabeth. He loved Bluebell ice cream, Dairy Queen Blizzards, and Subway cookies. He loved a piece of meat with his dessert. He loved sugars and hugs and saying "I Love You."

DENISE
He loved telling stories about his Granny, his parents, and his brothers. He loved Jesus and Charles Stanley. He loved First Baptist Groves and Leo Hebert. He loved us, and he loved his sons-in-law like they were his own boys. He loved his grandchildren. He loved our mom with his whole heart.

Our Daddy was full of life and full of love. His legacy will be the lessons of faith, faithfulness, hard work, and love he bestowed upon us. We will always be proud to be his daughters.

And in case you're wondering, Boudreaux said, "Dr. Trosclair. Marie's in labor. What do I do?" Dr. Trosclair asked, "Is this her first child?" Boudreaux answered, "No, stupid. This is her husband."

Chapter 25

What A Beautiful Day For A Funeral

After the funeral guests filed out of the room, we were alone with him. We had to say goodbye. I thought he looked good under the circumstances. I patted his now cold, hard hand. He was undoubtedly gone now. I smoothed his hair like I always did, but this time he didn't fuss at me for messing it up. I stared at him intently. I never wanted to forget his face. Not the one in pictures, but the one in my heart. They closed the lid to the coffin. I watched. I was numb. Now onto the cemetery.

I remember as he sat in Mom's car waiting for her to drive him to Penny's, just one week before, I thought it would be his last car ride. My error in thought was made abundantly clear as I watched his coffin through the back window of the hearse as we slowly made our way through the streets of Groves and into the cemetery. This was his final ride. This was final. The finale. The end.

We walked up to the gravesite and took our seats. The pall-bearers carried him respectfully and solemnly. The heaviness of this moment was wasted on none. The service was quick and sweet. My Uncle Pat, Daddy's oldest brother, was too weak from the effects of Parkinson's to walk up the inclined grass to the grave. Someone brought him a chair, and he sat, flanked by his other two brothers, and watched the final goodbyes. We hugged tightly and wished each other well as we went our separate ways. This turned out to be my Uncle Pat's final goodbye to us, as well. He passed away three months later.

It was a beautiful warm day. The perfect day for a funeral, or for hunting, or fishing, or golfing, or whatever Daddy would have wanted to do.

Chapter 26

I Am

I miss my Dad so much. I've missed him for several years, even though he's only been gone for a few short months. I miss his presence and his laugh and his cough. I know that sounds odd, but he coughed from smoking and allergies and when he laughed hard. I miss his cologne and his willingness to always help. I miss his recliner in Mom's den. I miss seeing him eating a burger, chips, and a root beer off the TV tray as he watched one of his favorite shows. I just miss him from that place between my heart and my throat. It tightens when I think about him.

My journey with him through this awful disease has been hard. Everyone who faces this has a different journey due to the relationship they have with their parent, the parent's personality, the way the disease affects the parent, and many other contributing factors. My sister and I had different journeys even though we were on the same path.

The one thing I am grateful for is his Strong Heart. I am grateful that he knew me on Wednesday afternoon before dreadful Thursday. I am grateful that he knew I was Denise and I was his oldest. I am grateful that he knew I loved him, and he loved me. I am grateful we got to have good-bye smooches one more lucid time. I am grateful I made it home before he died. I'm grateful I felt his last heartbeat and heard his last breath.

I'm grateful I was by his side as he stepped into glory. I know he will be by my side when I step out of this body and join him in heaven. I bet he will be laughing and smelling good.

Epilogue

Things I've Learned

What advice would I give someone starting this journey with their loved one?

Allow yourself to grieve as you go. You will be seeing changes and will miss who they were each step of the way.

Love them. If they are your parent, it's usually easy. I know there are people out there with a strained relationship with their parent. This may end up being a time of reconciliation. They need you.

Be patient. It's easy to become annoyed when they repeat themselves or act out in public or at home.

Tell them how proud you are of them. Chances are they tried to be a good parent. If they weren't, they may have done the best they could.

Treat them with dignity. Don't ask if they messed their pants or point out food on their face and shirt. Discreetly cover for them and clean them up. The old them would have never done such a thing.

Ask them if they can hold your hand and help you along. Hold their arm to "keep warm" rather than tell them they need help. Go along with the delusions if they are harmless. Agree that the sky is purple, and their truck was yellow. Why correct them? Pick your battles. There will be plenty to choose from.

Ask their opinion until they no longer have one. Don't talk about their shortcomings in front of them unless your doctor makes you. Then try to slip him a note or speak to his nurse. I think this is an awful practice. When they no longer remember you, remember them. I have been to visit my dad and my ex-mother-in-law, Fay, both in care facilities. My dad was happy to see me because he knew me. Fay was happy to see me, although she did not remember me. It was because I was friendly and talked to her. You only need to be kind.

Don't ask them to do things they can't do, like recall a name or tell a story. Don't say, "*I can't believe you don't remember that.*" They probably wish they did, but they don't.

Don't forget they are disabled. They look normal for most of the progress of the disease. Just because they can tell you "*No*" defiantly doesn't mean they are capable of making a wise decision as to whether to tell you "*No*" or not. They are not acting out on purpose. They might mean to do something, but they do not realize it is inappropriate. Part of their brain is dead. Not working. Gone. You wouldn't ask a person with one leg to run a marathon unless they had a prosthesis. There is no prosthesis or substitute for an Alzheimer's destroyed mind.

We would apologize to people if Daddy said or did something strange or mean or inappropriate. We would lean behind his back and say, "*He has Alzheimer's.*" He couldn't hear well, so it wasn't difficult. But I noticed that everyone was always kind. No one ever pointed or was rude to him. That may not be the case for everyone, but it was in our situation. I think it's because he smiled all the time.

What would I do differently? Spend more time with him. Take him to the woods. Take him to eat burgers. We did all those things, but I'd do them again if I could.

Recommended Books –

<u>Mayo Clinic On Alzheimer's Disease</u>, Ronald Petersen, M.D., Ph.D., Editor in Chief. Copyright 2002 Mayo Foundation for Medical Education and Research.

About The Author

Denise Carlin LeBlanc, the oldest of Ronnie Carlin's two daughters, was born and raised in Southeast Texas. Her heart's desire is to honor her father and to show who he was before and throughout his battle with this terrible disease. She also understands the value of faith, community and kindred-spirits in times of struggle.

Denise is the Chief Financial Officer for a Community Behavioral Health Center providing mental health, substance use, and intellectual and developmental disabilities services. She loves her job and is proud to work alongside extremely talented and caring people.

Denise LeBlanc was Shug to her Dad. She is Sweet Pea to her Mom. She is Mom to her daughter, Lauren and step-Mom to her two boys, Logan and Dylan. She is Maw Maw to her precious grandbabies, Connor and Stella. She's Dee to her sister, Julie and she is Darlin' to her always loving and supportive husband, Doug.

Endnotes

1. Reisberg, B., Ferris, S.H., de Leon, M.J., and Crook, T. The global deterioration scale for assessment of primary degenerative dementia. American Journal of Psychiatry, 1982, 139: 1136-1139.
2. Alzheimer's Association website. https://www.alz.org/alzheimers-dementia/stages, September 18, 2018.
3. Mayo Clinic website. https://www.mayoclinic.org/diseases-conditions/alzheimers-disease/in-depth/alzheimers-stages/art-20048448, September 18, 2018.
4. Mayo Clinic on Alzheimer's Disease. Published by Mayo Clinic Health Information, Rochester, Minn. Distributed to the book trade by Kensington Publishing Corporation, New York, N.Y. 2002. Mayo Foundation for Medical Education and Research. Page 9.
5. Alzheimer's Association website. https://www.alz.org/alzheimers-dementia/facts-figures. November 29, 2018.
6. https://www.betterhelp.com/advice/personality-disorders/inappropriate-affect-symptoms-and-signs/
7. https://www.mayoclinic.org/diseases-conditions/pseudobulbar-affect/symptoms-causes/syc-20353737
8. Reisberg, B., Ferris, S.H., de Leon, M.J., and Crook, T. The global deterioration scale for assessment of primary degenerative dementia. American Journal of Psychiatry, 1982, 139: 1136-1139.

[9] Mayo Clinic on Alzheimer's Disease. Published by Mayo Clinic Health Information, Rochester, Minn. Distributed to the book trade by Kensington Publishing Corporation, New York, N.Y. 2002. Mayo Foundation for Medical Education and Research.

[10] Mayo Clinic on Alzheimer's Disease. Published by Mayo Clinic Health Information, Rochester, Minn. Distributed to the book trade by Kensington Publishing Corporation, New York, N.Y. 2002. Mayo Foundation for Medical Education and Research. Page 37.

[11] Blood test detects Alzheimer's before symptoms appear, Published Monday 9 April 2018 Published Mon 9 Apr 2018 By Tim Newman , Fact checked by Honor Whiteman, https://www.medicalnewstoday.com/articles/321436.php. September 18, 2018.

[12] https://www.lifenph.com/about. November 29, 2018.

[13] Scripture quotations marked TPT are from The Passion Translation®. Copyright © 2017, 2018 by Passion & Fire Ministries, Inc. Used by permission. All rights reserved. ThePassionTranslation.com.

www.ingramcontent.com/pod-product-compliance
Lightning Source LLC
Chambersburg PA
CBHW060527080526
44586CB00012B/643